GAYATRI CHAKRAVORTY SPIVAK

Gayatri Chakravorty Spivak is one of the most influential figures in contemporary critical theory. However, her hugely important theoretical work is often hard to approach for the first time. This introduction offers a stepping stone to such crucial primary texts as *In Other Worlds* and *A Critique of Postcolonial Reason*.

Spivak is perhaps best known for her overtly political use of contemporary cultural and critical theories to challenge the legacy of colonialism on the way we read and think about literature and culture. Always cutting-edge, always provocative, Spivak champions the voices and texts of those marginalised by western culture and takes on many of the dominant ideas of the contemporary era. This volume examines her work through the issues of style, deconstruction, the subaltern, 'Third World' women and western feminism, materialism and value, postcolonialism and the literary text.

Anyone interested in contemporary cultural theory should read Gayatri Chakravorty Spivak. Any reader of Spivak should in turn look to this introduction.

Stephen Morton is Lecturer in English at Tampere University, Finland and has been a research fellow at the Whitney Museum of American Art Independent Study Program, New York City. He has published work on critical and cultural theory, twentieth-century literature and visual culture.

ROUTLEDGE CRITICAL THINKERS
essential guides for literary studies

Series Editor: Robert Eaglestone, Royal Holloway, University of London

Routledge Critical Thinkers is a series of accessible introductions to key figures in contemporary critical thought.

With a unique focus on historical and intellectual contexts, each volume examines a key theorist's:

* significance
* motivation
* key ideas and their sources
* impact on other thinkers

Concluding with extensively annotated guides to further reading, *Routledge Critical Thinkers* are the literature student's passport to today's most exciting critical thought.

Already available:

Roland Barthes by Graham Allen
Jean Baudrillard by Richard J. Lane
Simone de Beauvoir by Ursula Tidd
Maurice Blanchot by Ullrich Haase and William Large
Judith Butler by Sara Salih
Gilles Deleuze by Claire Colebrook
Jacques Derrida by Nicholas Royle
Michel Foucault by Sara Mills
Sigmund Freud by Pamela Thurschwell
Stuart Hall by James Procter
Martin Heidegger by Timothy Clark
Fredric Jameson by Adam Roberts
Julia Kristeva by Noëlle McAfee
Jean-François Lyotard by Simon Malpas
Paul de Man by Martin McQuillan
Friedrich Nietzsche by Lee Spinks
Paul Ricoeur by Karl Simms
Edward Said by Bill Ashcroft and Pal Ahluwalia
Jacques Lacan by Sean Homer
Slavoj Žižek by Tony Myers

For further details on this series, see www.literature.routledge.com/rct

GAYATRI CHAKRAVORTY SPIVAK

Stephen Morton

LONDON AND NEW YORK

First published 2003
by Routledge
2 Park Square, Milton Park, Abingdon, Oxon, OX14 4RN

Simultaneously published in the USA and Canada
by Routledge
270 Madison Avenue, New York, NY 10016

Reprinted 2005

Routledge is an imprint of the Taylor & Francis Group

© 2003 Stephen Morton

Typeset in Perpetua by
Florence Production Ltd, Stoodleigh, Devon
Printed and bound in Great Britain by
Biddles Ltd, King's Lynn, Norfolk

All rights reserved. No part of this book may be reprinted or reproduced or utilised in any form or by any electronic, mechanical, or other means, now known or hereafter invented, including photocopying and recording, or in any information storage or retrieval system, without permission in writing from the publishers.

British Library Cataloguing in Publication Data
A catalogue record for this book is available from the British Library.

Library of Congress Cataloguing in Publication Data
Morton, Stephen, 1972–
Gayatri, Chakravorty Spivak / Stephen Morton.
p. cm.– (Routledge critical thinkers)
Includes bibliographical references and index.
1. Spivak, Gayatri Chakravorty–Contributions in cultural studies. 2. Spivak, Gayatri Chakravorty–Contributions in feminist theory. 3. Spivak, Gayatri Chakravorty–Contributions in postcolonialism. 4. Spivak, Gayatri Chakravorty–Criticism and interpretation. I. Title. II. Series.

HV479.S65 M67 2002
306–dc21

2002068186

ISBN 0-415-22934-0 (hbk)
ISBN 0-415-22935-9 (pbk)

THIS BOOK IS DEDICATED TO
DAVID AND PATRICIA MORTON

CONTENTS

Series Editor's preface   ix
Acknowledgements   xiii

WHY SPIVAK?   1

KEY IDEAS   13
1   Theory, politics and the question of style   15
2   Setting deconstruction to work   25
3   Learning from the subaltern   45
4   'Third World' women and western feminist thought   71
5   Materialism and value   91
6   Colonialism, postcolonialism and the literary text   111

AFTER SPIVAK   135

FURTHER READING   143
Works cited   163
Index   171

SERIES EDITOR'S
PREFACE

The books in this series offer introductions to major critical thinkers who have influenced literary studies and the humanities. The *Routledge Critical Thinkers* series provides the books you can turn to first when a new name or concept appears in your studies.

Each book will equip you to approach a key thinker's original texts by explaining her or his key ideas, putting them into context and, perhaps most importantly, showing you why this thinker is considered to be significant. The emphasis is on concise, clearly written guides which do not presuppose a specialist knowledge. Although the focus is on particular figures, the series stresses that no critical thinker ever existed in a vacuum but, instead, emerged from a broader intellectual, cultural and social history. Finally, these books will act as a bridge between you and the thinker's original texts: not replacing them but rather complementing what she or he wrote.

These books are necessary for a number of reasons. In his 1997 autobiography, *Not Entitled*, the literary critic Frank Kermode wrote of a time in the 1960s:

> On beautiful summer lawns, young people lay together all night, recovering from their daytime exertions and listening to a troupe of Balinese musicians. Under their blankets or their sleeping bags, they would chat drowsily about the gurus of the time ... What they repeated was largely hearsay; hence my

lunchtime suggestion, quite impromptu, for a series of short, very cheap books
offering authoritative but intelligible introductions to such figures.

There is still a need for 'authoritative and intelligible introductions'. But
this series reflects a different world from the 1960s. New thinkers have
emerged and the reputations of others have risen and fallen, as new
research has developed. New methodologies and challenging ideas have
spread through the arts and humanities. The study of literature is no
longer – if it ever was – simply the study and evaluation of poems,
novels and plays. It is also the study of ideas, issues, and difficulties
which arise in any literary text and in its interpretation. Other arts and
humanities subjects have changed in analogous ways.

   With these changes, new problems have emerged. The ideas and
issues behind these radical changes in the humanities are often presented
without reference to wider contexts or as theories which you can simply
'add on' to the texts you read. Certainly, there's nothing wrong with
picking out selected ideas or using what comes to hand – indeed, some
thinkers have argued that this is, in fact, all we can do. However, it is
sometimes forgotten that each new idea comes from the pattern and
development of somebody's thought and it is important to study the
range and context of their ideas. Against theories 'floating in space', the
Routledge Critical Thinkers series places key thinkers and their ideas firmly
back in their contexts.

   More than this, these books reflect the need to go back to the
thinker's own texts and ideas. Every interpretation of an idea, even the
most seemingly innocent one, offers its own 'spin', implicitly or explicitly. To read only books on a thinker, rather than texts by that thinker,
is to deny yourself a chance of making up your own mind. Sometimes
what makes a significant figure's work hard to approach is not so much
its style or content as the feeling of not knowing where to start. The
purpose of these books is to give you a 'way in' by offering an accessible overview of these thinkers' ideas and works and by guiding
your further reading, starting with each thinker's own texts. To use a
metaphor from the philosopher Ludwig Wittgenstein (1889–1951),
these books are ladders, to be thrown away after you have climbed to
the next level. Not only, then, do they equip you to approach new ideas,
but also they empower you, by leading you back to theorist's own texts
and encouraging you to develop your own informed opinions.

   Finally, these books are necessary because, just as intellectual needs have changed, the education systems around the world – the contexts in which introductory books are usually read – have changed radically, too. What was suitable for the minority higher education system of the 1960s is not suitable for the larger, wider, more diverse, high technology education systems of the twenty-first century. These changes call not just for new, up-to-date, introductions but new methods of presentation. The presentational aspects of *Routledge Critical Thinkers* have been developed with today's students in mind.

Each book in the series has a similar structure. They begin with a section offering an overview of the life and ideas of each thinker and explain why she or he is important. The central section of each book discusses the thinker's key ideas, their context, evolution and reception. Each book concludes with a survey of the thinker's impact, outlining how their ideas have been taken up and developed by others. In addition, there is a detailed final section suggesting and describing books for further reading. This is not a 'tacked-on' section but an integral part of each volume. In the first part of this section you will find brief descriptions of the thinker's key works: following this, information on the most useful critical works and, in some cases, on relevant websites. This section will guide you in your reading, enabling you to follow your interests and develop your own projects. Throughout each book, references are given in what is known as the Harvard system (the author and the date of a work cited are given in the text and you can look up the full details in the bibliography at the back). This offers a lot of information in very little space. The books also explain technical terms and use boxes to describe events or ideas in more detail, away from the main emphasis of the discussion. Boxes are also used at times to highlight definitions of terms frequently used or coined by a thinker. In this way, the boxes serve as a kind of glossary, easily identified when flicking through the book.

The thinkers in the series are 'critical' for three reasons. First, they are examined in the light of subjects which involve criticism: principally literary studies or English and cultural studies, but also other disciplines which rely on the criticism of books, ideas, theories and unquestioned assumptions. Second, they are critical because studying their work will provide you with a 'tool kit' for your own informed critical reading and thought, which will make you critical. Third, these thinkers are critical because they are crucially important: they deal with ideas and questions which can overturn conventional understandings of the world, of texts, of everything we take for granted, leaving us with a deeper understanding of what we already knew and with new ideas.

No introduction can tell you everything. However, by offering a way into critical thinking, this series hopes to begin to engage you in an activity which is productive, constructive and potentially life-changing.

ACKNOWLEDGEMENTS

Many thanks to the artists, curators and scholars of the Whitney Museum of American Art Independent Study Program 2000–2001, to Bob Eaglestone and Liz Thompson for all the hard work on the series, to Rene Gabri, Ayreen Anastas and the Sixteen Beaver Street Reading Group, to the staff and students at the Department of English, University of Tampere, to Susan Bennett, Ron Clark, Jeff Derksen, Esther Gabara, Alia Hasan Khan, Lynette Hunter, Pat Maniscalco, Ashok Mathur, David Murray, Kamran Rastegar, David Robertson, Andrew Ross, Neluka Silva, Jon Simons, Aruna Srivastava, and to Susan Kelly for her loving intellectual support. Finally, an apology to Gayatri Spivak. I hope that this systematic and at times reductive presentation of a much more complex and sophisticated body of work will, at the very least, provide a point of entry into some of the most important and engaging social and political thought of our time.

WHY SPIVAK?

Gayatri Chakravorty Spivak is best known for her overtly political use of contemporary cultural and critical theories to challenge the legacy of colonialism on the way we read and think about literature and culture. What is more, Spivak's critical interventions encompass a range of theoretical interests, including Marxism, feminism, deconstruction, postcolonial theory and cutting-edge work on globalisation. Along with other leading contemporary intellectuals such as Edward Said and Homi Bhabha, Spivak has challenged the disciplinary conventions of literary criticism and academic philosophy by focusing on the cultural texts of those people who are often marginalised by dominant western culture: the new immigrant, the working class, women and the postcolonial subject.

By championing the voices and texts of such minority groups, Spivak has also challenged some of the dominant ideas of the contemporary era. Such ideas include, for example, the notion that the western world is more civilised, democratic and developed than the non-western world, or that the present, postcolonial era is more modern and progressive than the earlier historical period of European colonialism in the nineteenth century.

Indeed, for Spivak the effects of European colonialism did not simply vanish as many former European colonies achieved national independence in the second half of the twentieth century. Rather, the social, political and economic structures that were established during colonial rule continued to inflect the cultural, political and economic life of post-colonial nation states ranging from Ireland to Algeria; from India to Pakistan and Jamaica to Mexico. In common with many anti-colonial intellectuals, including Frantz Fanon (1925–61) and Partha Chatterjee (1947–), Spivak emphasises how anti-colonial nationalism assumed a distinctively bourgeois character, and was thus perceived by many to reproduce the social and political inequalities that were predominant under colonial rule. Spivak further suggests that the emergence of the United States of America as a global economic super-power in the latter half of the twentieth century has redrawn the old colonial maps in the interests of multinational corporate finance and on the backs of 'Third World' women.

Taken together, what these critical interventions collectively demonstrate is the importance of reading Gayatri Spivak. For there are few other contemporary intellectuals who have managed to sustain a sophisticated engagement with contemporary critical and cultural theory, while always grounding that intellectual engagement in urgent political considerations about colonialism, postcolonialism and the contemporary international division of labour between the 'First World' and the 'Third World'.

GAYATRI CHAKRAVORTY SPIVAK

Spivak's intellectual work has been shaped by the experience of post-colonial migration from India to the USA, where she currently teaches. In *The Post-Colonial Critic* (1990), Spivak identifies herself as a postcolonial intellectual caught between the socialist ideals of the national independence movement in India and the legacy of a colonial education system. In a profound moment of self-parody, Spivak compares herself to the drunken father in Hanif Kureishi's play about South Asian immigrants living in Britain, *My Beautiful Launderette*, because this character 'uses an outdated "socialist" language in a colonial accent' (Spivak 1990: 69).

Gayatri Chakravorty Spivak was born in Calcutta on 24 February 1942, the year of the great artificial famine and five years before independence from British colonial rule. She graduated from Presidency College of the University of Calcutta in 1959 with a first-class honours degree in English, including gold medals for English and Bengali literature. In this respect, her education could be regarded as a legacy of the colonial education policies that had been in place in India since the days of the British Empire in the nineteenth century.

The colonial administrator and English historian Thomas Babington Macaulay (1800–59) had written in the early nineteenth century of how the British Empire's policies on education in India encouraged educated, middle-class Indian subjects to internalise the cultural values of the British. For Macaulay and other British colonial bureaucrats of the time, the teaching of British cultural values to the upper middle class in India was intended to instruct and enlighten the Indian middle class in the morally and politically superior culture of the British Empire. By employing such policies and practices, the British tried to persuade the Indian middle class that colonial rule was in its best interests.

For Spivak, the teaching of English literature in colonial India provided an insidious, though effective way of executing the civilising mission of imperialism. Spivak's literary criticism has worked to criticise this ideological function of English literature in the colonial context. In 'Three Women's Texts and a Critique of Imperialism' (1985) for example, Spivak contends that 'It should not be possible to read nineteenth-century British literature without remembering that imperialism, understood as England's social mission, was a crucial part of the cultural representation of England to the English' (Spivak 1985: 243).

Spivak left India for the USA in 1959 to take a Masters' degree at Cornell University, followed by a year's fellowship at Girton College, Cambridge, England. Nevertheless, the intellectual tradition of left-wing, anti-colonial thought that was prevalent in India since the early twentieth century continued to tacitly influence Spivak's work. As the influential postcolonial critic Robert Young emphasises, Spivak's thought is best understood if it is situated in terms of ongoing political debates within India about the employment of classic European Marxism in the context of anti-colonial struggles, and the failure of Indian socialism to recognise the histories and struggles of women, the underclass, the tribal communities and the rural peasantry in Indian society (Young 2001: 350–52).

After completing the fellowship in England, Spivak subsequently returned to the USA to take up an instructor's position at the University of Iowa, while completing a doctoral dissertation on the work of the Irish poet W.B. Yeats (1865–1939), which was being directed by the literary critic Paul de Man (1919–83) at Cornell University, New York state.

THE POLITICS OF DECONSTRUCTION

Along with the French philosopher Jacques Derrida (1930–), Spivak's professor Paul de Man was one of the most prominent and rigorous advocates of deconstruction in North America during the 1960s and 1970s (see box on Derrida and deconstruction, pp. 26–7). De Man's approach to reading emphasised how the meaning of a literary text is not stable or transparent, but is radically indeterminate and therefore always open to further questioning. For de Man, the practice of literary criticism is not a matter of formulating a single, correct interpretation; instead, de Man argues that texts contain blind spots which always and necessarily lead to errors and misreadings.

De Man's deconstructive criticism has certainly influenced Spivak's early readings of British colonial archives and official Indian historiography; her readings of William Wordsworth's *The Prelude*, Virginia Woolf's *To the Lighthouse* and the works of W.B. Yeats; as well as her groundbreaking translation and scholarly preface to Jacques Derrida's *Of Grammatology*. For some readers, Spivak's allegiance to deconstruction might at first seem surprising when one considers Spivak's overtly political commitment to champion the cause of minority groups. After all, the deconstructive assertion that the meaning of a text is radically unstable and indeterminate would also surely weaken the effectiveness of any political intervention?

For Spivak, however, the popular understanding of deconstruction as apolitical and relativist is both reductive and simplistic. From the outset, Spivak has persistently and persuasively demonstrated that deconstruction is a powerful political and theoretical tool. One of the ways in which Spivak has demonstrated the political value of deconstruction is by focusing on the rhetorical blind spots or grounding mistakes which stabilise conventional notions of truth and reality. Along with other key figures such as Jacques Derrida, Ernesto Laclau, and Edward Said, Spivak has foregrounded the textual elements that shape our understanding of the social world, and thereby questioned the binary opposition between philosophical or literary texts and the so-called real world.

Like Said and Derrida, Spivak has examined the way in which the real world is constituted by a network of texts, from British colonial archives to US foreign policies, computerised stock exchange market reports and World Bank Reports on the 'Third World' debt. In doing so, Spivak has increasingly sought to challenge some of the dominant ideas about contemporary globalisation. One such idea is that the new speed and flexibility of technology enables the effective transnational circulation of people, money and information. This dominant idea clearly ignores the fact that the circulation of money and information is profitably regulated by rich, industrial 'First World' nations, while the vast majority of the world's population are living in a state of poverty and oppression.

By highlighting the political and economic interests which are served by the economic text of globalisation, Spivak exposes how the world is represented from the dominant perspective and geopolitical location of the 'First World' to the exclusion of other disenfranchised groups. Such a radical challenge to the truth claims of western democracy and globalisation has expanded the focus of deconstruction from the textual analysis of literature or philosophy to include the contemporary economic and political text. As I will go on to argue, this change in focus also highlights the political consequences of all reading practices.

THE QUESTION OF STYLE

Spivak's attempt to map the effects of different colonial legacies to the way we think about contemporary cultural objects and everyday life is often presented in a complex language and style that may at first appear difficult, and can be off-putting to some readers approaching her work for the first time. What is more, this difficult prose style may seem to contradict the overt political aim of Spivak's work: to articulate the voice and political agency of oppressed subjects in the 'Third World'.

Like many other thinkers of the twentieth century, including the German philosopher Theodor Adorno (1903–69) in particular, Spivak crucially challenges the common-sense assumption that clear, transparent language is the best way to represent the oppressed. In fact, Spivak suggests that the opposite is actually true. For the transparent systems of representation through which things are known and understood are also the systems which control and dominate people. For this reason, Spivak's thought emphasises the limitations of linguistic and philosophical representation, and their potential to mask real social and political inequalities in the contemporary world. As Spivak states in an interview:

> [W]hen I'm pushed these days with the old criticism – 'Oh! Spivak is too hard
> to understand!' – I laugh, and I say okay. I will give you, just for your sake, a
> monosyllabic sentence, and you'll see that you can't rest with it. My monosyl-
> labic sentence is: *We know plain prose cheats.*
>
> (Danius and Jonsson 1993: 33)

Spivak's statement that 'plain prose cheats' clearly illustrates how the basic syntactic structure of the 'monosyllabic sentence' is contradicted by the semantic content of the sentence. Yet the point that Spivak is trying to convey in this example is not simply a play with words. Far from simply presenting her arguments in inaccessible prose, Spivak's essays and books carefully link disparate histories, places and method-ologies in ways that often refuse to adhere to the systematic conventions of western critical thought. Such a refusal to be systematic is not merely a symptom of current academic or theoretical fashion, but a conscious rhetorical strategy calculated to engage the implied reader in the crit-ical interrogation of how we make sense of literary, social and economic texts in the aftermath of colonialism.

SUBALTERN STUDIES

Over fifty years after the declaration of India's national independence from British colonial rule, one of the most important political ques-tions that Spivak's work asks is why nationalism has failed to represent the majority of India's population. During the struggle for national independence in India, the nationalist political figure Mohandas Karamchand Gandhi (1869–1948) had led a policy of passive resistance against the British. This policy mobilised the popular political support of subaltern groups (see box, p. 48), including the rural peasantry and women in a practice of *satyagraha*, or feminised non-violent struggle. There are numerous other examples of subaltern resistance to colonial rule and class oppression from the eighteenth century onwards, but these are largely unrecorded in the annals of official history.

As Spivak emphasises, the work of the Subaltern Studies historians has sought to correct the class and gender blindness of elite bourgeois national independence in India by re-writing history from below. For Subaltern Studies historians such as Ranajit Guha (1923–), the national independence movement ultimately conserved the existing class struc-ture in India: leaving a small group of educated, middle-class men holding political and economic power, and a large impoverished population of rural-based peasant labourers, with little or no access to the benefits of national independence. Spivak has developed the ideas of the Subaltern Studies historians further, emphasising that the western Marxist model of social change that these historians employ does not do justice to the complex histories of subaltern insurgency and resistance which they seek to recover.

This critique of the Subaltern Studies historians exemplifies how Spivak has relentlessly questioned the ability of western theoretical models of political resistance and social change to adequately represent the histories and lives of the disenfranchised in India. More specifically, Spivak has argued that the everyday lives of many 'Third World' women are so complex and unsystematic that they cannot be known or represented in any straightforward way by the vocabularies of western critical theory. In this respect, the lived experiences of such women can be seen to present a crisis in the knowledge and understanding of western critical theory (Hitchcock 1999: 65). For Spivak, this crisis in knowledge highlights the ethical risks at stake when privileged intellectuals make political claims on behalf of oppressed groups. These risks include the danger that the voices, lives and struggles of 'Third World' women will be silenced and contained within the technical vocabulary of western critical theory.

Such an awareness of the ethical risks involved in postcolonial theory is not merely self-defeating, however. In her writings on Mahasweta Devi's fiction, for example, Spivak frequently engages with the singular histories and lives of 'Third World', subaltern women in order to disrupt the codes and conventions of western knowledge and the maintenance of imperial power.

SPIVAK AND FEMINISM

As I suggested, Spivak has further expanded the historical research of the Subaltern Studies historians by focusing on the experiences of subaltern women, which have been effaced in official Indian history. In 'A Literary Representation of the Subaltern' (1988) Spivak argues that the Bengali language fiction writer Mahasweta Devi (1926–) powerfully articulates the history of subaltern women through her female protagonist, Jashoda, in the story 'Breast Giver'. The story depicts the decay of Jashoda's maternal body after she is employed as a professional mother in a wealthy Brahmin household. For Spivak, Jashoda's brutal-ised maternal body powerfully highlights the failure of Indian national-ism to emancipate lower-class, subaltern women, and also challenges the assumption, predominant in western society and culture, that women's reproductive labour is unwaged, domestic work.

Another crucial contribution to feminist thought that Spivak has made is the critique of western feminism, especially its universalising claim to speak for all women, regardless of differences in class, religion, culture, language or nationality. As a young Indian woman starting a career in the US academy in the late 1960s, Spivak describes how femi-nism was 'the best of a collection of accessible scenarios' (Spivak 1987: 134). Yet despite this general leaning towards western feminism, Spivak has questioned the 'lie' of a global sisterhood between 'First World' and 'Third World' women, pointing instead to the complicity of western feminism and imperialism. By doing so, Spivak expands and complicates the critical terms and political objectives of feminism in a way that is more sensitive to questions of difference.

One of the major challenges facing Spivak is whether talking about these issues in an academic setting will make any difference to the lives and experiences of the disempowered, subaltern groups she describes. Throughout her work, Spivak is constantly critical of her own pos-ition as an educated, middle-class professor, who now holds a chair at Columbia University in New York City. What is more significant, however, is the way in which Spivak talks about her location as a middle-class Indian migrant intellectual in the US academy. As the con-temporary cultural critics Aijaz Ahmad, Arif Dirlik and Rey Chow have emphasised, the rise of postcolonial studies in the US academy is co-extensive with US foreign policy and economic investment in the 'Third World'. This historical parallel might suggest that postcolonial studies indirectly serve the interests of US foreign policy and global economic expansion by producing knowledge about the 'Third World'. To counter this difficulty, Spivak persistently emphasises how in her own critical thought she resists the temptation to appear as a spokesperson or native informant for the 'Third World' in the 'First World' academy, even though she acknowledges that the position of a famous postcolo-nial intellectual who lives and works in the western metropolitan academy and champions the cause of minority groups is a position that is beset with contradiction and paradox.

SPIVAK'S KEY IDEAS

For Spivak, the traditional disciplines of rational academic inquiry have restricted the way we think about texts and ideas in relation to the social, political and economic world. Before we can learn anything about the economic text of globalisation or the patriarchal oppression of 'Third World' women, Spivak insists that we must first unlearn the privileged systems of western knowledge that have indirectly served the interests of colonialism and neo-colonialism.

Spivak's thought traverses a range of critical theories, texts and contexts which overlap and intricate in illuminating and radical ways. It would thus be impossible to reduce Spivak's thinking to a single critical position. Instead, the Key Ideas section traces the evolution of Spivak's most important interventions in a way that is in keeping with the political spirit and theoretical complexity of her thought.

Chapter 1 starts off by looking at Spivak's aphoristic and provisional style of writing. Situating Spivak's style in relation to poststructuralist debates about the relationship between the text and the world, this chapter considers how Spivak's style of writing resists the temptation to represent oppressed minorities in a transparent discourse that has traditionally denied their voice and agency.

Chapter 2 examines the influence of deconstruction on Spivak's thought and traces Spivak's inventive use of deconstruction from the 'Translator's Preface' to Derrida's *Of Grammatology* (1976) to 'The Setting to Work of Deconstruction' (1998). Against the charge that Spivak's work is opaque and inaccessible, this chapter considers how Spivak has changed the emphasis of deconstruction by focusing her critical attention on contemporary political concerns such as globalisation and the international division of labour.

Discussion then turns to the intellectual and theoretical sources that have influenced Spivak's writings about the subaltern. After a consideration of Spivak's reading of the Subaltern Studies historical research, Chapter 3 proceeds to examine Spivak's most famous and controversial essay, 'Can the Subaltern Speak?' (1988; first published in 1985). To set this essay in context, the chapter initially considers Spivak's critique of representation in the work of French intellectuals Michel Foucault (1926–84) and Gilles Deleuze (1925–95). Then, the chapter moves on to look at the representation of widow sacrifice in the nineteenth-century colonial archives and the Hindu texts of antiquity. Finally, the chapter examines what is at stake in Spivak's provocative assertion that 'there is no space from which the sexed subaltern can speak' (Spivak 1988: 308).

Chapter 4 continues the discussion of the subaltern woman by focusing on Spivak's contribution to feminism. 'French Feminism in an International Frame' (1981) is perhaps Spivak's clearest argument against the colonial benevolence of western feminism. In this essay, Spivak criticises Julia Kristeva's (1941–) arrogant focus on the European feminist self in the book *About Chinese Women* (1977). Kristeva's discussion of female sexuality in *About Chinese Women* is also the occasion for Spivak's rethinking of female clitoridectomy as the symbolic condition of all women's social and economic oppression. This thread is continued in 'Three Women's Texts and a Critique of Imperialism' (1985), where Spivak considers how Charlotte Brontë's narrative of female individualism, *Jane Eyre* (1847), is predicated on the erasure of the colonial woman, Bertha Mason. As Spivak suggests, there are important lessons that contemporary western feminist thought can learn and unlearn from the proto-feminist literary narratives of British colonialism.

Chapter 5 turns to Spivak's rethinking of Marx and value. This aspect of Spivak's work is often overlooked because it is based on Marx's later economic writings. Yet a basic understanding of Marx is absolutely crucial to an understanding of Spivak's ideas. The chapter begins by situating Spivak's engagement with Marx in relation to contemporary re-readings of Marx. Focusing on 'Scattered Speculations on the Question of Value' (1985) the chapter moves to consider how Spivak has reconsidered Marx's writings on value as deconstructive before their time. Such a re-thinking of Marx's writings on value, labour and capitalism has transformed the contemporary understanding of materialist thought. What is more, Spivak's re-reading of Marx demonstrates the continuing importance of Marx's critique of capitalism to the political and economic legacy of colonialism, globalisation and the international division of labour.

Chapter 6 considers Spivak's contribution to colonial discourse studies and postcolonial theory. Beginning with an examination of Spivak's argument that English literature aided and abetted the civilising mission of colonialism, the chapter proceeds to consider Spivak's readings of Charlotte Brontë's *Jane Eyre* and Immanuel Kant's *Critique of Judgement* (1790). The chapter then considers Spivak's critique of postcolonial texts. It is now commonplace in postcolonial literary criticism to argue that postcolonial texts such as Jean Rhys's (1894–1979) *Wide Sargasso Sea* (1966) and J.M. Coetzee's (1940–) *Foe* (1986) subvert the originary master narratives of colonialism by rewriting them. Spivak questions this common view, arguing that the exaggerated political claims made on behalf of postcolonial texts often ignore how postcolonial societies are still riven by the legacy of colonialism. As a counterpoint to these political claims, Spivak's commentaries and translations of the Bengali language writer Mahasweta Devi have forcefully articulated the material reality of postcolonial nationalism from the embodied standpoint of tribal, subaltern women.

The final chapter of this book, 'After Spivak', addresses Spivak's impact in the field of critical theory and the unparalleled influence that Spivak's work has had in the field of postcolonial theory. Over the past twenty years, Spivak's thought has had an increasing impact in discussions about feminism, the future of Marxism after the collapse of Soviet communism, and the impact of global capitalism. In this way, Spivak has expanded the horizons of an increasing intellectual effort to critically assess the cultural and political legacy of colonialism in the contemporary world.

In the final Further reading section of this book, I offer a guide and bibliography for those wondering where they might begin in the important task of reading Spivak's works and those of her critics.

KEY IDEAS

KEY IDEAS

1

THEORY, POLITICS AND THE QUESTION OF STYLE

One of the most important contributions that Spivak has made to contemporary critical thought is in the effective re-working of western theoretical concepts and ideas to address contemporary political concerns in the postcolonial world. It is this persistent endeavour to make western critical theory account for contemporary forms of political, economic and social inequality and oppression in the contemporary world that makes Spivak's thought particularly engaging and valuable.

In a detailed critical overview of Spivak's work, the postcolonial literary critic Bart Moore-Gilbert (1997) argues that Spivak, along with Edward Said and Homi Bhabha, has been one of the foremost figures to accommodate ideas and concepts from western critical theory within the field of postcolonial studies. As Moore-Gilbert further notes, however, this application of western critical theory has had a mixed reception. For some critics of postcolonial theory, including Aijaz Ahmad and Arif Dirlik, the use of western critical theory in postcolonial thinking represents a new form of intellectual colonialism, which is politically complicit with global capitalism. For more sympathetic commentators, such as Robert Young, however, the rise of postcolonial theory in the western academy cannot be separated from important debates among politicians and intellectuals in the 'Third World' during the 1960s and 1970s about the limitations of nationalism and Marxism as effective models of political emancipation.

THE WORLDLINESS OF THE TEXT

Robert Young's argument that postcolonial theory is part of the larger social and historical context in which it is written recalls Edward Said's earlier contention in *The World, the Text, the Critic* (1983) that 'all texts are worldly, even when they appear to deny it, they are nevertheless a part of the social world, human life, and of course the historical moments in which they are located and interpreted' (Said 1983: 4). For Said, one of the most important signs of a text's worldliness is its style: 'the recognizable, repeatable, preservable sign of an author who reckons with an audience [. . .] style neutralises the worldlessness, the silent, seemingly uncircumscribed existence of a solitary text' (Said 1983: 33). In Said's account, style should directly reflect a writer's engagement with the social and historical world. What is more, Said attacks the 'difficult' style or jargon of contemporary literary theory on the grounds that it 'obscures' social reality and 'encourage[s] a scholarship of "modes of excellence" very far from daily life' (Said 1983: 4).

If Said attacks the jargon of literary theory on the grounds that it alienates the non-specialist reader and retreats from the social and historical world, Spivak's style of composition might at first seem to confirm Said's argument against literary theory. For Spivak's notoriously difficult style of composition has vexed even supposed affiliates of literary theory such as the British Marxist literary critic Terry Eagleton. In a devastating review of Spivak's book *A Critique of Postcolonial Reason* (1999), Eagleton has charged Spivak with deliberate theoretical obscuritanism, metaphorical muddles and heavy-handed jargon. Eagleton's overtly hostile review certainly identifies some of the stylistic difficulties that readers of Spivak's work might encounter, but it does little to elucidate the important intellectual histories and theoretical discourses that inform much of Spivak's writing.

In a more careful reading of Spivak's work Bart Moore-Gilbert observes how Spivak frequently employs a 'provisional and informal mode of composition' (Moore-Gilbert 1997: 76). Such a mode of composition should not be taken as a sign that Spivak's work is simply opaque or lacking in intellectual rigour, however. From the outset, Spivak's work has critically engaged with some of the most difficult European philosophical discourse, including texts by Immanuel Kant (1724–1804), George Wilhelm Friedrich Hegel (1770–1831),

Karl Marx (1818–83), Sigmund Freud (1856–1939), Jacques Derrida (1930–) and Michel Foucault (1926–84).

What is more, Spivak's critical engagement with the deconstructive philosopher Jacques Derrida (discussed in Chapter 2) has problematised the neat binary opposition between the text and the world, which informs Edward Said's critique of deconstruction in *The World, the Text, the Critic*. In a response to Said's work published in 'Can the Subaltern Speak?', Spivak takes issue with Said's assertion that 'Derrida's criticism moves us *into* the text, Foucault's *in* and *out*' (Spivak 1988: 292). For Spivak, Said constructs a false dichotomy between the text and the world, which Said attributes to the 'criticism' of Jacques Derrida and Michel Foucault respectively. Furthermore, Spivak argues that Said's statement betrays 'a profound misapprehension of the notion of textuality' (292).

TEXTUALITY AND WORLDING

Spivak's criticism of Said in turn reveals how Jacques Derrida's deconstruction of the binary opposition between the text and the world has perhaps been most influential in shaping the compositional style and rhetoric of Spivak's thought. Writing in France during the late 1950s and early 1960s, Jacques Derrida challenged the structuralist idea, developed first by the Swiss linguist Ferdinand de Saussure (1857–1913), and then later by the French literary critic Roland Barthes (1915–80) and the French anthropologist Claude Lévi Strauss (1908–), that one could study language scientifically as a structure of 'signs', made up of 'signifiers' (e.g. a word) and 'signifieds' (that to which the signifier refers). The meaning we take from a signifier relies on certain conventions: a dog is not inherently a 'dog', but rather we recognise that the word 'dog' signifies that particular animal. A green light means 'go' only within a certain (arbitrary) system. Crucially, signification works through difference: a thing is defined in relation to what it is not. A dog is not a cat, for example, and a green light (go) is not a red light (stop). Following Saussure's argument in *Course in General Linguistics* that 'in language there are only differences without positive terms (1959: 120)', Derrida challenged the scientific claims of early structuralism, emphasising instead that language is a system of differences in which signification or meaning is perpetually deferred, and cannot be reduced to any structure. What is more, Derrida argued that language does not transparently reflect the social and historical world. As Derrida asserts in *Of Grammatology* (1976), 'there is nothing outside of the text' (Derrida 1976: 163).

This statement has been the source of much controversy because it appears to deny that there is a real world outside of language. But this interpretation of Derrida's statement grossly misrepresents Derrida's position. What is crucial for Derrida is that there is no essential difference between language and the world. For the very terms 'language' and 'world' are themselves privileged signs that are part of a larger, irreducible system of linguistic and non-linguistic 'marks'. Instead, writing in general, or textuality, refers to the endless series of marks or traces that is a necessary condition of all signifying systems. (Chapter 2 examines Derrida's 'poststructuralist' thought in more detail.)

Derrida's early work on writing and textuality has been particularly important to Spivak because it throws into question the common-sense assumption that there is a stable and transparent correspondence between language and the so-called real world. For Spivak, one of the main problems with this transparent model of language is that it has been variously used to represent and constitute the world as a stable object of western knowledge. As Spivak emphasises in an interview with Elizabeth Grosz, this transparent representation of the world is bound up with the history of European imperial expansion from nineteenth-century British colonialism to twentieth-century US foreign policy-making, the development policies of the World Bank and the World Trade Organisation. Spivak refers to this dominant representation of the world as 'worlding', or 'the assumption that when the colonizers come to a world, they encounter it as uninscribed earth upon which they write their inscriptions' (Spivak 1990: 129).

Spivak's discussion of worlding serves to illustrate how she carefully elaborates the usefulness of poststructuralist concepts such as textuality for contemporary postcolonial thinking. I will go on to explain the political importance of deconstruction for Spivak's engagements with postcolonial and Marxist thinking more fully in later chapters. The remaining part of this chapter will suggest that the 'fragmentary and provisional' style of Spivak's writing reflects a political commitment to describing the conditions of oppression and exploitation under contemporary global capitalism, without jeopardising the complexity of particular theoretical arguments.

WORLDING, TEXTUALITY AND THE DISCOURSE OF COLONIALISM

The term 'worlding' in Spivak's work refers to the way in which writing in general, or textuality, has provided a rhetorical structure to justify imperial expansion. In many literary, historical, legal and geographical texts written during the colonial period, such as William Shakespeare's play *The Tempest*, the archives of the East India Company or David Livingstone's nineteenth-century African travel journals, there are frequent references to colonial territories as empty, uninscribed land or *terra nullius*; or to indigenous peoples without culture, writing or political sovereignty. These descriptions of colonial territory as uninscribed earth, and of indigenous communities as peoples without writing and political sovereignty, are persuasive metaphors employed to justify colonial expansion. Indeed, what these metaphors illustrate is how people and territory have been controlled, subjected, dispossessed and exploited through dominant systems of western writing, textuality and knowledge. As Spivak puts it:

> As far as I understand it, the notion of textuality should be related to the notion of the worlding of a world on a supposedly uninscribed territory. When I say this, I am thinking basically about the imperialist project which had to assume that the earth that it territorialised was in fact previously uninscribed.
>
> (Spivak 1990: 1)

At times, Spivak also uses the related term epistemic violence to emphasise how western knowledge or epistemology has been used to justify the violent exercise of political and military force over other non-western cultures. This relationship between western knowledge and the violence of colonial dispossession is illustrated in the following passage from Joseph Conrad's novel *Heart of Darkness* (1902):

> The conquest of the earth, which mostly means the taking it away from those who have a different complexion or slightly flatter noses than ourselves, is not a pretty thing when you look into it too much. What redeems it is the idea only.
>
> (Conrad [1902] 1973: 10)

Conrad's correlation of the violent exercise of colonial dispossession and the redemptive 'idea' of imperialism as a civilising mission illustrates the damaging effects that western knowledge continues to have on non-western cultures. For in emphasising the moral and intellectual superiority of western culture, Europeans were able to justify the violent project of imperialist expansion as a civilising mission.

CRITICAL INTERRUPTIONS

As suggested in 'Why Spivak?' (see pp. 5–6), Spivak's resistance to the clarity of style associated with 'plain prose' is a conscious decision calculated to engage an implied reader in the self-conscious interroga-tion of how we make sense of literary, social and economic texts in the historical aftermath of colonialism. In Spivak's account, the style or presentation of theoretical ideas should reflect the contradictory and overdetermined character of social and geopolitical relations rather than obscuring them. For this reason, Spivak's 'difficult' style of com-position should be considered as an inextricable part of her theoretical method.

In the preface to *In Other Worlds*, Spivak's first collection of essays, Colin MacCabe describes Spivak as a 'feminist Marxist deconstructivist' (Spivak 1987: ix). Far from adhering rigorously to the terms or concepts of any one theoretical method, Spivak's work frequently emphasises the limitations and blind spots of academic disciplinary discourse. In an interview with Elizabeth Grosz, Spivak rejects the idea of reconciliation between Marxism, feminism and deconstruction on the grounds that such totalising theoretical models are 'too deeply marked' by 'colo-nialist influence' (Spivak 1990: 15). Instead, Spivak asserts that 'the irreducible but impossible task is to preserve the discontinuities within the discourses of feminism, Marxism and deconstruction' (Spivak: 1990: 15). Spivak has subsequently referred to this task as the 'critical interruption' of Marxism, feminism and deconstruction (Spivak 1990: 110). As I go on to suggest below, this intellectual practice of inter-ruption and negotiation is better understood if it is placed in the context and tradition of the 'Third World' political thought of (for example) Mohandas Karamchand Gandhi (1869–1948) and Frantz Fanon (1925–61). Gandhi and Fanon started the revision and adaptation of western political thought in the context of 'Third World' national liberation struggles earlier in the twentieth century.

Spivak's strategy of critical interruption can be briefly illustrated by a comparison of her theoretical arguments in different critical essays. In 'Scattered Speculations on the Question of Value' (1985), Spivak emphasises the importance of Marx's labour theory of value for thinking about the international division of labour between the 'Third World' and the 'First World'. Yet in 'Feminism and Critical Theory' (1978) and 'A Literary Representation of the Subaltern' (1988) Spivak criticises Marx's labour theory of value because it ignores the unwaged productive and reproductive labour power of women in the 'Third World'. (Marx's theory will be discussed in more detail in Chapter 4; see box, p. 101) Just so, in 'French Feminism in an International Frame' (1981) and 'Imperialism and Sexual Difference' (1986) Spivak accuses western feminism of ignoring the plight of 'Third World' women.

What is more, Spivak acknowledges how deconstruction can operate as a critical safeguard against the utopian promises that feminism and Marxism makes to oppressed groups in the 'Third World'. Yet at the same time, Spivak questions the radical political claims that have been made on behalf of western poststructuralism. In 'Can the Subaltern Speak?', for instance, Spivak criticises Michel Foucault's theoretical model of power/knowledge (discussed in Chapter 3) for ignoring the international division of labour, and the continued exploitation of 'Third World' workers both at home and abroad (Spivak 1988: 289). And in 'Ghostwriting' (1995), Spivak argues that Jacques Derrida is unable to comprehend the systematic character of an emergent global capitalism because Derrida misunderstood Marx's central argument about industrial capitalism in *Capital Volume Two*.

Robert Young in *White Mythologies* (1990) further counters the charge of difficulty and elitism made against Spivak by the Marxist critic Terry Eagleton and others. In Young's argument, the difficulty of Spivak's work does not arise in the style of composition *per se*, but in the refusal to reconcile the differences, or discontinuities, between the critical vocabularies of Marxism, feminism and deconstruction. As Young states:

> Instead of staking out a single recognisable position, gradually refined and developed over the years, [Spivak] has produced a series of essays that move restlessly across the spectrum of contemporary theoretical and political concerns, rejecting none of them according to the protocols of an oppositional

mode, but rather questioning, reworking and reinflecting them in a particularly productive and disturbing way.

(Young 1990: 157)

Whereas Spivak's more severe critics attribute the complexity of Spivak's writing to a lack of coherence or to impatience with deliberate conceptual refinement, Young situates Spivak's complex theoretical 'position' in the historical context of 'Third World' political thought. As I go on to suggest in later chapters, Spivak's rethinking of feminism, Marxism and deconstruction is informed by the crucial ethical and political imperatives of oppressed, subaltern groups living in the 'Third World'.

For Spivak, the need to rework these different methodologies in the contemporary 'Third World' context highlights the particular limitations of Marxism and feminism as conceptual blueprints for social change. In this respect, Spivak's thought is torn between the demands for theoretical rigour and political commitment. As Rey Chow asserts in a reading of Spivak's engagement with Marx:

The problem is that, caught between the deconstructive demand to be nuanced with regard to textual heterogeneity [. . .] and the rationalist demand to be 'vigilant' to 'errors' committed exploitatively against the disenfranchised, Spivak's writing must become more and more 'self-conscious' – self-referential and self-subverting at once – even as, ironically, some of her readers charge her for being too theoretical and elitist (i.e., deconstructionist) while others criticize her for being heavy-handed (i.e., not paying enough attention to the fine turns of philosophical texts).

(Chow 1998: 40)

This tension between the demands for political commitment on the one side and theoretical or philosophical rigour on the other can be traced back to Karl Marx's assertion in 'The Eleventh Thesis on Feuerbach' (1845) that: 'The philosophers have only ever interpreted the world, the point however is to change it' (Marx 1977: 158).

From one point of view, Spivak may certainly be regarded as a meticulous 'interpreter' or reader of several important European philosophers and thinkers. Spivak's translation and preface to Jacques Derrida's *Of Grammatology* are now required reading for any serious Derrida scholar, and her graduate seminars on the original German language edition of Karl Marx's *Das Kapital* have gained legendary status at Columbia University, New York (where Spivak currently teaches).

Yet Spivak is more than just a rigorous commentator on western critical theory. In a paper on Jacques Derrida's work, entitled 'Touched by Deconstruction' and presented at the Angel Orensantz Foundation, New York City (2000), Spivak underlined the necessity – originally articulated by Jacques Derrida – for slow and careful reading at a time of political urgency. Such a statement may seem to confirm Spivak's allegiance to Derrida's deconstruction of western philosophical and political thought. Yet, at the same time, Spivak does not always strictly adhere to the philosophical terms in which Derrida's thought is read and discussed. Like many other intellectuals of the late twentieth century, including Theodor Adorno and Frantz Fanon, as well as the recent 'internationalist' thought of Jacques Derrida, Spivak has pushed against the narrow, hermetic focus of western philosophy to demonstrate the worldliness of critical theory. What is more, Spivak's theoretical interventions persistently interrupt the rigorous conventions of western critical thought to articulate the continued exploitation of subaltern groups in the 'Third World'.

SUMMARY

- The fragmentary and provisional style of Spivak's theoretical writing can be seen as a rhetorical strategy which is employed to highlight the limitations and openings that are specific to the political programmes of Marxism, feminism and nationalism.

- Spivak's rhetorical strategy can be seen to expand and develop earlier debates about the relevance and pragmatic value of western political thought in the context of 'Third World' liberation struggles, and in their aftermath.

- Spivak's approach to style differs strikingly from that of the postcolonial intellectual Edward Said, who argues that the 'difficult' style or jargon of contemporary literary theory 'obscures the social realities that [. . .] encourage a scholarship of "modes of excellence" very far from daily life' (Said 1983: 4). By contrast, Spivak suggests that the style of theoretical composition should be complex and flexible enough to reveal the complex, contradictory and shifting status of social and geopolitical relations.

- Spivak's style might also be regarded as a sign of Spivak's own worldliness: as a theorist who occupies the paradoxical position of championing the voices and struggles of the oppressed in the 'Third World' in a necessarily complex theoretical vocabulary, and from a relatively privileged location inside the western academy.

2

SETTING
DECONSTRUCTION
TO WORK

As suggested in the previous chapter, one of the most important conceptual sources for the development of Spivak's ideas is the work of the Algerian-born French philosopher, Jacques Derrida (1930–). From the outset, Derrida has questioned the truth claims of western philosophy by emphasising how the coherence and stability of traditional philosophical concepts such as consciousness, being or knowing depend on a system of differences or binary oppositions. These oppositions might include presence/absence, speech/writing, or self/other, for example. This chapter will look quite closely at Spivak's readings of Derrida and will also touch upon other critics' responses to his work in order to place Spivak's readings in a certain intellectual and political context. This emphasis should not in any way suggest that Spivak is only important as a 'reader of Derrida'. Her work on Derrida – not least her translation of and preface to his *Of Grammatology* – has certainly played a vital role in presenting his thought to an English-speaking audience. However, what is most important in this chapter, and throughout the rest of the book, is the original way in which Spivak expands Derrida's deconstructive thinking beyond the framework of western philosophy, and sets it to work in diverse fields ranging from 'Third World' women's political movements to postcolonial literary studies and development studies.

Before turning to Spivak's deployment of deconstruction, it is important to examine the 'basics' of Derrida's deconstructive strategies.

DERRIDA AND DECONSTRUCTION

Deconstruction is a strategy of critical analysis developed by the French philosopher Jacques Derrida in dialogue with the history of western philosophy. Typically, commentators have struggled to define deconstruction because it cannot be reduced to a method, or defined as a theory with a clear set of objectives. This point is reiterated in Derrida's 'Letter to a Japanese Friend': 'Deconstruction is not a method and cannot be transformed into one' (Derrida 1991: 4).

Nevertheless, there are key points and moments throughout Derrida's work where the critical strategies of deconstruction can be traced. One of the first instances of deconstruction is seen in Derrida's essay 'Différance' (1967). Following the work of the Swiss linguist Ferdinand de Saussure (1857–1913), Derrida argues in this essay that the process of making meaning (signification) is structured in terms of how signs *differ* from other signs: a thing is defined in relation to what it is not. So, for example, presence is defined by its difference from non-presence; 'me' is defined by its difference from 'you'; 'here' is defined by its difference from 'there'; 'civilised' is defined by its difference from 'savage'; and 'West' is defined by its difference from 'East'. Taking Saussure's argument a step further, however, Derrida emphasised that meaning is always *perpetually deferred* across a spatial and temporal axis, so that a final point of stable meaning and knowledge is never reached in any signifying system. Derrida's contention that meaning is radically unstable is demonstrated in the very title word of his essay 'Différance': for the French verb *différer* means both to differ and to defer.

Another word for '*différance*' is supplement. In Derrida's view, linguistic (and non-linguistic) signs are never fully identical with the things they refer to; indeed, signs are structurally incomplete from the beginning, and thus require additional or supplementary terms to complete them. The need for supplementation to compensate for the lack of original self-identity thus reveals how all linguistic or non-linguistic signs are by definition incomplete and lacking in identity or self-presence. In this way, Derrida's thought radically undermines the authority and centrality of the western humanist subject, epitomised in René Descartes' statement that 'I think therefore I am'.

Derrida further emphasises that the repression, exclusion and erasure of 'impossible' concepts such as *différance* and the supplement from the history of western philosophy are also the very conditions of possibility which ground and constitute philosophical meaning and truth. A clear example of this is seen in Derrida's discussion of the experience of death in *Aporias* (1993). In this book Derrida traces the impossibility of representing the particular experience of death in the positive terms of language and philosophical conceptuality. In Derrida's terms, the singular experience of death and dying is an *aporia*, or a double bind which cannot be presented in the logical terms of western philosophy. Yet at the same time, it is precisely the singular experience of death that defines the contours of being, existence and consciousness. Indeed, death is precisely that which remains unthought in the western philosophical terms of being and self-presence. In other words, death can be regarded as a *constitutive* aporia, because it provides the unrepresentable ground against which being, existence and self-presence are defined and thereby constituted.

Derrida's deconstructive strategies have been particularly generative for postcolonial intellectuals such as Homi Bhabha, Robert Young and Gayatri Spivak because they provide a theoretical vocabulary and conceptual framework to question the very philosophical tradition that has also explained and justified the subjection, dispossession, and exploitation of non-western societies. Spivak has carefully followed the trajectory of Jacques Derrida's thought from his early deconstruction of western philosophy to more recent discussions of ethics, justice, post-Marxist ideas of internationalism, friendship and hospitality. In doing so, Spivak has stressed the potential usefulness of Derrida's thought for making effective critical interventions in the discourse of colonialism, the contemporary global economy, and the international division of labour between the 'First World' and the 'Third World'.

THE 'TRANSLATOR'S PREFACE' TO *OF GRAMMATOLOGY*

Spivak's 'Translator's Preface' to *Of Grammatology* (1976) was written at a time when Jacques Derrida's work was not widely known, or understood, in the English-speaking world of philosophy and literary criticism. In the preface, Spivak offers a comprehensive account of the key philosophical debates that influenced Derrida's early work, as well as providing an intellectual context for Derrida's deconstructive philosophy. Spivak offers relevant and illuminating commentaries on key nineteenth-

and twentieth-century critical interventions: Friedrich Nietzsche's critique of truth, Sigmund Freud's theory of memory and the unconscious, Edmund Husserl's phenomenology, Martin Heidegger's engagement with the question of being, and Emmanuel Levinas's rethinking of ethics, as well as the structural linguistics of Ferdinand de Saussure, Roland Barthes and Claude Lévi Strauss, the psychoanalysis of Jacques Lacan and the discourse analysis of Michel Foucault. By doing so, Spivak challenges the conventions and expectations of a 'Translator's Preface' to produce a scholarly and critical introduction to Derrida's deconstructive philosophy that is equal to many of the subsequent philosophical commentaries that have been published about Derrida's thought.

Certainly, Spivak's 'Translator's Preface' to *Of Grammatology* anticipates some of the questions and debates addressed in the critical scholarship about Derrida, in the work of current critics and thinkers, such as, for example, Geoffrey Bennington, Simon Critchley, Rodolphe Gasché, Marian Hobson and Christopher Norris. Yet, the trajectory of Spivak's subsequent critical engagement with Derrida's thought differs significantly from the more orthodox philosophical readings of Derrida, exemplified in the work of these thinkers. As I go on to suggest below, Spivak has mobilised Derrida's deconstruction of western philosophy to expand and develop debates among 'Third World' intellectuals about the cultural legacy of colonialism; the ability of western Marxism to describe the continued exploitation of 'Third World' workers by 'First World' multinational corporations; and the question of whether western feminism is appropriate to describe the histories, lives and struggles of women in the 'Third World'.

DECONSTRUCTION AND THE POSTCOLONIAL CONTEXT

In an interview with Elizabeth Grosz, Spivak situates her political interest in Derrida's thought in relation to her earlier experience of the British colonial education system in India. Spivak writes:

> Where I was brought up – when I first read Derrida I didn't know who he was, I was very interested to see that he was actually dismantling the philosophical tradition from *inside* rather than *outside*, because of course we were brought up in an education system in India where the name of the hero of that philosophical system was the universal human being, and we were taught that if we could

begin to approach an internalisation of that human being, then we would be
human. When I saw in France someone was actually trying to dismantle the
tradition which had told us what would make us human, that seemed interesting too.

(Spivak 1990: 7)

Spivak's interest in Derrida's intellectual project is not merely philosophical, but is also partly motivated by a desire to 'dismantle' the very
tradition of western thought that had provided the justification for
European colonialism. Indeed, as Spivak suggests, Derrida's deconstruction of the western humanist subject can also be productively
employed in the context of postcolonial thought.

Such an argument is echoed in Robert Young's *White Mythologies*.
In Young's view, the development of many French poststructuralist
theories was informed and influenced by the Algerian war of independence (1954–62) (Young 1990: 1). For many French intellectuals,
including Jacques Derrida, the Algerian war of independence was an
important reminder of how the freedom, or sovereignty, of the human
subject in western liberal democracies such as France was secured
through colonial exploitation and capitalist expansion in other parts
of the world. In short, the freedom and sovereignty of the human
subject in the 'First World' was predicated on the oppression and
exploitation of colonial subjects in the 'Third World'. As a consequence,
the possibility of universal human rights, freedom and equality as a
political goal, as well as a philosophical foundation, was radically thrown
into question. Like Spivak, Young convincingly demonstrates how
Derrida's deconstruction of western thought can be related to the recent
history of decolonisation and anti-colonial resistance. At times, however, Young exaggerates the significance of Derrida's biography, as a
Franco-Maghrebian Jew, who was born in Algeria, in order to
strengthen his argument that deconstruction is an essential part of postcolonial intellectual history. Yet as Spivak emphasises, the details of
Derrida's early life in Algeria are not '"postcolonial" in any precise
sense' (Spivak 1999: 431).

In the postcolonial theory of Homi Bhabha, Jacques Derrida's discussion of *différance* has provided a radical conceptual resource to deconstruct the rhetoric of colonial discourse. In response to Derrida's
discussion of the differing–deferral of signs along an infinite space–
time axis, Homi Bhabha has suggested that the 'structure' of colonial

discourse takes place along a parallel axis of enunciation (the context of utterance) and address (the context of listening). In 'Sly Civility' (1994), Bhabha examines a speech delivered by the British thinker John Stuart Mill (1806–73) to a select committee of the English House of Lords in 1852 about the British colonial government in India. In this speech, Mill states that the maintenance of colonial government takes place in and through writing, or the letters, documents, records and policies that are exchanged between the British government in London and the colonial administration in India. Against the colonial authority implicit in Mill's speech, Bhabha argues that the 'space between enunci-ation and address' – between London and India – 'opens up a space of interpretation and misappropriation that inscribes an ambivalence at the very origins of colonial authority' (Bhabha 1994: 95). By doing so, Bhabha emphasises that the very structure of colonial address provides a rhetorical space for potentially subverting the authority of colonial rule in writing.

Bhabha's inventive use of Derrida's discussion of *différance* in the context of nineteenth-century British colonial discourse is paralleled by his employment of the deconstructive concept of the *supplement* to rewrite the fixed narratives of contemporary western nation states such as Britain and France from the perspective of postcolonial migrants. In 'DissemiNation', Bhabha uses Derrida's 'wit and wisdom' (1994: 139) to challenge the conventional Eurocentric narrative of the western nation. Invoking *Handsworth Songs*, a film made by the Black Audio and Film Collective during the uprisings of 1985 in the Handsworth area of Birmingham, England, Bhabha traces a split in the film's narrative between the racist discourses of British state institutions in statistics, documents and newspapers, and 'the perplexed living' of postcolonial migrants dwelling in Britain which is expressed in 'Handsworth songs' (Bhabha 1994: 156). For Bhabha, films such as *Handsworth Songs* illus-trate how the coherent, linear narrative of the modern western nation state is interrupted by its own colonial history, which it tries desper-ately to disavow and forget. As Bhabha asserts:

> The liminality of the western nation is the shadow of its own finitude: the colo-nial space played out in the imaginative geography of the metropolitan space; the repetition or return of the postcolonial migrant to alienate the holism of history. The postcolonial space is now 'supplementary' to the metropolitan centre; it stands in a subaltern, adjunct relation that doesn't aggrandize the

presence of the West but redraws its frontiers in the menacing, agonistic boundary of cultural difference that never quite adds up [. . .].

(Bhabha 1994: 168)

In the last sentence of this quoted passage, Bhabha uses the critical strategies of deconstruction to emphasise the structural incompleteness of white British national culture from the position of new immigrant populations from Africa, the Caribbean and South Asia. Just as Jacques Derrida's supplement highlights the original incompleteness of western philosophy, so the postcolonial migrant foregrounds and challenges the incomplete cultural identity of British nationhood from a vulnerable position on the margins of the nation (Bhabha 1994: 168).

Bhabha's deconstruction of the discourse of the western nation state from the perspective of new immigrants has provided a powerful model for rethinking the cultural identity of western nation states such as Britain. Yet Bhabha's generalisations about the experiences of post-colonial migrants often fail to take into account the important economic, political and class differences between these postcolonial migrants. As a consequence, Bhabha often implies that his own position as a privileged postcolonial intellectual, who emigrated from India to live in Britain and then the USA, is interchangeable with the material conditions of other immigrants, such as Turkish labourers living in Germany, or the African-Caribbean community depicted in *Handsworth Songs*. In contrast to Bhabha, Spivak acknowledges the privileged middle-class position that she occupies as a postcolonial intellectual in the western academy, but also emphasises that this space is produced by western higher educational institutions funded by multinational capitalism.

DECONSTRUCTION AND OTHER WORLDS

The articulation of deconstruction and postcolonial theory in the work of Young and Bhabha is prefigured in Spivak's 1976 'Translator's Preface' to *Of Grammatology*. In this preface, Spivak emphasises that the conceptual organisation of Derrida's book has a 'geographical pattern' (Derrida 1976: lxxxii), wherein the deconstruction of *western* philosophy (in the first part of the book) is indirectly related to the critique of western anthropology (in the second part). This relationship becomes more explicit in the second section of Derrida's book, entitled 'The

Violence of the Letter', where Derrida carefully traces the ethnocentric blind spots in 'A Writing Lesson', an essay written by the French
anthropologist Claude Lévi Strauss (1908–). In this essay, Lévi Strauss
describes how he conducted detailed anthropological fieldwork with
the Nambikwara, an oral-based tribal society in South America. After
completing his fieldwork, Lévi Strauss concluded that this society
represented an innocent people untouched by civilisation because they
were without writing. For Derrida, however, this sentimental characterisation of the Nambikwara reproduces a cultural stereotype of
indigenous people as noble savages, and thereby ignores the complex
and situated textual practices that had been historically employed in the
Nambikwara society.

Derrida's critique of Lévi Strauss illustrates how the invocation of
the non-west in recent western critical theory is often employed as a
rhetorical gesture to mark the limitations of western knowledge. Such
a rhetorical gesture often portrays non-western subjects as petrified,
mute objects of western representation who are denuded of culture,
language and history. This depiction of non-western subjects at the
unrepresentable limits of knowledge may guard against the utopian
claims of political programmes such as Marxism or national independence, which claim to represent the interests of disempowered or
oppressed groups. Yet critical theory's emphasis on the silence and
passivity of non-western subjects in relation to western knowledge
also re-focuses attention on the conceptual limitations of *western* knowledge itself. For the postcolonial critic Homi Bhabha this problem is part
of western theory's 'strategy of containment where the Other text is
forever the exegetical horizon of difference, never the active agent of
articulation' (Bhabha 1994: 31).

At times, Spivak's emphasis on the complicity of western intellectuals in silencing the voices of oppressed groups by speaking for them
may also appear to repeat the very silencing that Bhabha criticises above.
Indeed, critics such as Benita Parry argue that Spivak effectively writes
out 'the evidence of native agency recorded in India's 200 year struggle
against British conquest and the Raj' (Parry 1987: 35) with phrases like,
'The subaltern cannot speak' (Parry 1987: 35). As I go on to discuss in
Chapter 3, Parry's reading of Spivak's work on the subaltern exemplifies how many critics have tended to oversimplify Spivak's argument for
the sake of clarity. Far from being completely pessimistic about the
histories of subaltern resistance and the possibilities of political agency,

Spivak's refusal to simply represent non-western subjects comes from a profound recognition of how the lives of many disempowered groups have already been damaged by dominant systems of knowledge and representation. And it is deconstruction that provides Spivak with a critical strategy to articulate this recognition.

In 'Can the Subaltern Speak?', for example, Spivak invokes the history of Bhubaneswari Bhaduri, a young, middle-class, Indian woman who took her own life in her father's apartment in North Calcutta in 1926. It was later discovered that this woman was a 'member of one of the many groups involved in the armed struggle for Indian independence' (Spivak 1988: 307). As Spivak goes on to point out, Bhubaneswari had been 'entrusted with a political assassination', which she was unable to confront, and had committed suicide to avoid capture by the British colonial authorities. Spivak reads Bhubaneswari's suicide as an elaborate attempt to cover up her involvement with the anti-colonial insurgency movement by disguising her suicide as a modern example of the ancient practice of Hindu widow sacrifice (discussed in more detail in Chapter 3). Yet in doing so, Spivak argues that the voice and agency of Bhubaneswari Bhaduri, as a real historical woman and an anti-colonial freedom fighter, disappear from the official, male-centred historical records.

In the conclusion to the reading of Bhubaneswari Bhaduri's suicide, Spivak argues that Jacques Derrida provides a 'more painstaking and useful' way of reading the voices and struggles of disenfranchised subjects such as Bhubaneswari Bhaduri (Spivak 1988: 308). Rather than perpetuating Bhubaneswari's disappearance from history, such a reading practice allows Spivak to be more self-conscious, self-subverting and ethically responsible in the way that she talks about the singular experiences and histories of disenfranchised people like Bhubaneswari in her own theoretical discourse.

DECONSTRUCTION AND MASTERWORDS

The disappearance of Bhubaneswari Bhaduri from the historical records of anti-colonial insurgency also highlights a more general problem with the vocabularies of political movements such as anti-colonial national liberation, feminism or socialism. These movements attempt to name and define the particular histories, experiences and struggles of minority groups using abstract master words like the worker, the woman or the

CATACHRESIS

In the study of rhetoric, the term *catachresis* denotes the misuse or abuse of words to 'name the multiplicities of experience and environment under broader, single signs' (Wales 1989: 57–8). In Jacques Derrida's deconstruction of western philosophical discourse, however, *catachresis* is not restricted to the particular misuse of words, but refers instead to the original incompleteness or impropriety that is a general condition in all systems of meaning. In the English language, for example, the proper name 'Jeff Derksen' is supposed to correspond with a real concrete person, but there is no absolute guarantee that the proper name 'Jeff Derksen' refers to the same person, or that the person is the same as they were two weeks ago. As Geoffrey Bennington notes in a lucid commentary on Derrida's work, the 'proper name ought to insure a certain passage between language and the world, in that it ought to indicate a concrete individual, without ambiguity, without having to pass through the circuits of meaning' (Bennington 1993: 104). Yet as Bennington goes on to point out, the identity of the proper name with a 'concrete individual' is also grounded on the repression of non-identity, or impropriety: '[the] proper name and proper meaning are only distinguished in secondary fashion against a background of originary impropriety or metaphoricity' (Bennington 1993: 107). As Bennington suggests, the impropriety of the proper name refers to the more general condition of impropriety, which underpins all systems of meaning.

colonised. Spivak contends that these master words are catachreses, or improper words, because they claim to represent all women, all workers and all of the proletariat, when 'there are no "true" examples of the "true worker," the "true woman," the "true proletarian" who would actually stand for the ideals in terms of which you've mobilized' (Spivak 1990: 104).

Jacques Derrida's deconstruction of the proper/improper dichotomy in western philosophical discourse has had a significant influence on Spivak's thinking, especially in the reworking of Marxist and feminist concepts. In an interview with Sarah Harasym, entitled 'Practical Politics of The Open End' (1990), Spivak acknowledges that Derrida's deconstruction of western metaphysics 'cannot found a political program of any kind [. . .] Yet, in its suggestion that masterwords like "the worker", or "the woman" have no literal referents deconstruction is [a] political safeguard' (Spivak 1990: 104). For Spivak, the 'political' value of a deconstructive reading practice is that it guards against the universal claims of Marxism, national liberation movements or western feminism to speak for all the oppressed.

In the context of political mobilisation, the use of master words is catachrestic not only because it is improper in grammatical or logical terms, but also because it can have an abusive effect on those people, whose lives and experiences are named and defined by such master words. As Spivak emphasises in 'Can the Subaltern Speak?' (1988), the voice of 'the worker' or 'the woman' in political discourse is often represented by a political proxy, or an elected representative, who speaks on behalf of these constituencies. Such political discourses tend to represent these disempowered groups as if they were speaking collectively as a unified political subject. For Spivak, however, this coherent political identity is always already an effect of the dominant discourse that represents these groups, rather than a transparent portrait of the true worker, or the true woman. (I will return to the question of discourse in Chapter 3; see box, p. 85.)

Spivak's reworking of deconstruction in the context of political representation illustrates how the language of universal political struggles can have potentially injurious or harmful effects on the lives of disempowered groups (the colonised, women, or the workers). The example of Bhubaneswari Bhaduri, discussed above, illustrates how the complex lives, histories and struggles of the disempowered can be erased by the fixed terms of radical political discourses that claim to represent them. To counter this difficulty, Spivak argues that Derrida offers a more flexible and responsible approach to reading the singular circumstances and material conditions of people's lives, which 'marks radical critique with the danger of appropriating the other by assimilation' (Spivak 1988: 308). As the next section considers, this responsible approach, which Spivak finds in Derrida's deconstruction of western philosophy, reflects a more general concern in Derrida's later work to rethink ethics as a responsibility towards the Other.

DECONSTRUCTION AND ETHICS

At a conference entitled 'The Ends of Man' held at the Centre Culturel International de Cerisy-La-Salle, France in 1980, Spivak, along with other key commentators on Derrida's thought including Jean Luc Nancy, Phillipe Lacoue Labarthe and Sarah Kofman, met to discuss the question of politics and the status of the political in Jacques Derrida's thought. The proceedings from this conference were published in French under the title, *Les fins de l'homme: à partir du travail de Jacques Derrida* (1981), and have not yet been translated, although some of the presentations have been discussed in subsequent publications. In 'Limits and Openings of Marx in Derrida', an essay published in *Outside in the Teaching Machine* (1993), Spivak notes how the opening conference discussions of Derrida's work were structured around a binary opposition between the two most common meanings of the political in French: *le politique*, or the abstract philosophical notion of the political, and *la politique*, or the more conventional definition of politics as a concrete political event.

In Spivak's account, this binary opposition, originally proposed by Jean-Luc Nancy and Phillipe Lacoue Labarthe, is problematic because it presents deconstruction as an abstract philosophical method which is divorced from the material conditions of concrete political events. Instead of simply framing the relationship between deconstruction and politics in the reductive terms of this binary opposition between political philosophy and real, material politics, Spivak suggests that we should examine the difference between Derrida's early and later work more carefully.

In Derrida's early work, Spivak asserts that there is 'an economy [. . .] of protecting and preserving [*garder*] the question' whereas in the later work there is a 'transformation' of this economy of protection and preservation into 'the call to the wholly other [*tout autre*]' (Spivak 1993: 98–9). In more simple terms, there is a movement in Derrida's thought away from major philosophical questions about the founding conditions of possibility for truth, being ('ontology') and knowing ('epistemology') towards ethical and social considerations about violence, justice, friendship, and hospitality. As I go on to discuss below, Spivak's focus on this move in Derrida's work clarifies the meaning of the political in Derrida's thought, and reveals instead how Derrida's deconstruction of western philosophy has an important ethical dimension that persistently questions the rational programmes which structure all political decision-making.

Derrida's preoccupation with ethics has been implicit in his thinking from the start of his intellectual career, even though, as Geoffrey

Bennington (2000) stresses, deconstruction is not ethical in the conventional sense of the term. Traditionally, ethics belongs to the realm of moral philosophy concerned with the calculation of justice. In this tradition, ethics is bound up with the transcendent, universal principles of western metaphysics; the very principles that deconstruction seeks to deconstruct (Bennington 2000: 64).

Instead of articulating a coherent moral philosophy, Derrida bases his understanding of ethics on the thought of the Jewish philosopher Emmanuel Levinas (1906–95). The clearest statement of Levinas's ethical position can be found in his book *Totality and Infinity* (1961). In this book, Levinas redefined ethics as the moment in which the transcendental self of western philosophy discovers that it is already in an ethical relation to the Other before it is fully a self. Indeed for Levinas, ethics is nothing more than the singular event in which the Self encounters itself in an ethical relation to the face of the Other.

OTHERNESS

Throughout the history of western culture and thought, there are certain people, concepts, and ideas that are defined as 'Other': as monsters, aliens or savages who threaten the values of civilised society, or the stability of the rational human self. Such 'Others' have included death, the unconscious and madness, as well as the Oriental, non-western 'Other', the foreigner, the homosexual, and the feminine. In the structure of western thought, the 'Other' is relegated to a place outside of or exterior to the normal, civilised values of western culture; yet it is in this founding moment of relegation that the sovereignty of the Self or the same is constituted. The challenge that otherness or alterity poses to western thought and culture has been further developed by Emmanuel Levinas. For Levinas, western philosophy has traditionally defined the Other as an object of consciousness for the western subject. This reductive definition has effectively destroyed the singular alterity of the Other. Against this reduction, Levinas has asserted that the Other always escapes the consciousness and control of the western self. For Levinas, the challenge that the alterity of the Other poses to the certainty of the Self in the face-to-face encounter between the Self and the Other opens the question of ethics.

The theme of Otherness has also been a central concern in post-colonial studies. In the introduction to *Orientalism*, Edward Said argued that the Orient is one of Europe's 'deepest and most recurring images of the Other' (Said 1978: 1). Whereas Said describes how Orientalism controls the non-western world by defining it as the Other of Europe, Spivak has tried to displace this fixed Self–Other dichotomy in favour of an ethical response to the lives and struggles of oppressed people in the 'Third World'. This intellectual endeavour is painstaking and difficult, and has led Spivak to refer to ethics as an experience of the impossible (Spivak 1995: xxv).

For Jacques Derrida, the problem with Levinas's thought is that there is no guarantee that an ethical relation will take place in the singular event of the face-to-face encounter between the Self and the Other. After all, what is there to prevent the self from exploiting, injuring, or even killing the Other? This difficulty is further compounded in the attempt to find an appropriate way to respond to the Other. As Simon Critchley observes in a commentary on Derrida's rethinking of ethics, the 'attempt to articulate conceptually an experience that has been forgotten or exiled from philosophy can only be stated within philosophical conceptuality, which entails that the experience succumbs to and is destroyed by philosophy' (Critchley 1992: 94). For Critchley, the very possibility of responding to the Other in an ethically responsible way is always threatened by the risk that the singular voice and experience of the Other might be destroyed. Yet, on the other hand, the vulnerable process of articulating such an experience may also transform the structure of self-centred philosophical discourse in a way that recognises Otherness.

This is one of the chances that deconstruction takes. By questioning the founding conditions of possibility that make western philosophical discourse intelligible, Derrida also traces the 'Other' experiences, histories, cultures and people that western philosophy has at various points tried to exclude, silence and destroy. The problem facing Derrida, however, is that there are no guarantees that this ethics of reading will not fall prey to the very structures of violence that it attempts to escape from. Rather than denying this risk of complicity, however, Derrida affirms this risk at the forefront of his interventions. As Derrida states in *Of Grammatology*:

> Operating necessarily from the inside, borrowing all the strategic and economic
> resources from the old structure, borrowing them structurally, that is to say
> without being able to isolate their elements and atoms, the enterprise of decon-
> struction always in a certain way falls prey to its own work.
>
> (Derrida 1976: 24)

For Derrida, any attempt to define the founding conditions of philosophical truth from a purely objective position *outside* of philosophical
discourse is necessarily doomed to fail. Instead, Derrida concentrates
on the more modest task of inhabiting the structures of philosophical
texts in order to trace those figures, histories and people who have been
excluded from western philosophical discourse as its founding condition
of possibility.

DECONSTRUCTIVE READING IN SPIVAK'S THOUGHT

For Spivak, deconstruction's affirmation of the complicity of theory
with its object of critique is the 'greatest gift' of deconstruction because
it 'question[s] the authority of the investigating subject without para-
lysing him' (Spivak 1987: 201). For this reason, Spivak repeats
Derrida's strategy of reading with literary and historical discourses to
trace the founding exclusions inherent in radical political programmes
such as Marxism, decolonisation or feminism.

For example, in 'A Literary Representation of the Subaltern' (1988),
Spivak questions the socialist, democratic promises made to the people
by leaders of the anti-colonial resistance movement during the struggle
for national independence in India. More specifically, Spivak suggests
that the mythology of Mother India that was invoked by anti-colonial
insurgents (including Gandhi) during and after the struggle for national
independence perpetuated the rigid class system established under
the British Empire, and ignored the plight of lower-caste, subaltern
women. To challenge the class-based structure of this nationalist
mythology, Spivak performs a textual analysis of 'Breast Giver', a short
story by the Bengali-language fiction writer, Mahasweta Devi. In this
story, the female protagonist, Jashoda, a subaltern woman, is hired by
a wealthy Brahmin family as a professional mother. The story narrates
the subsequent grotesque putrefaction of Jashoda's maternal body
after breast-feeding several high-caste, Brahmin children. For Spivak,

Jashoda's diseased, exploited and lower-caste maternal body highlights the limitations of the Mother India mythology as a bourgeois ideological construct. Against the democratic promises of the anti-colonial nationalist movement to transform the rigid class structure in India, Spivak emphasises that lower-caste women like Jashoda have been effectively excluded from the foundations of national independence. In the deconstructive terms of Spivak's argument, the exploitation of Jashoda's lower-caste, maternal body emphasises how decolonisation falls prey to and replicates the very colonial structures of class and gender oppression it claims to oppose.

Another instance where Spivak employs a deconstructive approach to political programmes is in the essay 'Imperialism and Sexual Difference' (1986). In this essay, Spivak criticises some western feminists for ignoring the specific experiences of 'Third World' women when they construct a universal feminist subject. It is in this context that Spivak asserts that 'varieties of feminist criticism and practice must reckon with the possibility that, like any other discursive practice, they are marked and constituted by, even as they constitute, the field of their production' (Spivak 1986: 225). Put more simply, western feminist criticism has tended to focus on the exclusion of women from the 'masculist truth-claim to universality or academic objectivity' (Spivak 1986: 226). Yet this focus repeats the universalist errors of masculine-centred truth claims or objective knowledge by suggesting that all women the world over suffer from the same sort of oppression simply because they are women. Indeed, Spivak contends that western feminism has itself fallen prey to its own work by claiming to speak for all women, when it often excludes the experiences of 'Asian, African [and] Arab' women (Spivak 1986: 226). Against this 'lie' of 'global sisterhood', Spivak has thus criticised western feminism for ignoring the plight of 'Third World' women (Spivak 1986: 226). Again, this critique of western feminism demonstrates the value of deconstruction as an ethical reading practice, which emphasises the risk of political complicity with dominant social and political structures as a necessary part of all intellectual practices.

Some critics of Spivak's work are sceptical of whether Spivak's deconstructive reading strategies achieve anything other than a theoretical paralysis of effective political intervention. In a critical reading of Spivak's work, Asha Varadharajan has argued that Spivak's 'unremitting exposure of complicity' (Varadharajan 1995: 89) actually prevents Spivak from articulating moments of political resistance. Invoking

Spivak's discussion of Bhubaneswari Bhaduri's suicide in 'Can the Subaltern Speak?' (discussed above on p. 33), Varadharajan contends that Spivak's account of Bhaduri's struggle is encumbered by a reliance on Derridian deconstruction. Instead, Varadharajan suggests that Spivak's thinking can be 'redeemed' through a focus on the work of the twentieth-century German philosopher Theodor Adorno (1903–69).

In Varadharajan's argument, Adorno's resistance to the transparent presentation of philosophical concepts in writing has given way to a mode of composition that struggles to present social relations in fragments, aphorisms and paratactic phrases (where one proposition is placed after another, without indicating relations of coordination or subordination between them) (Varadharajan 1995: 78). Furthermore, Adorno's use of chiasmus, or the grammatical figure whereby the order of words in one clause is inverted in a second clause, aims to provide readers with a glimpse of the concrete historical conditions and material relations which are distorted by western knowledge and cognition. For example, the statement, 'the subject is the object, the object is the subject' demonstrates how the object of thought is determined by the investigating subject. In the case of western knowledge produced about the non-western world the object of thought disappears under the weight of western representation. For Varadharajan, Adorno's thought provides a way out of this dilemma because it can differentiate between the 'concreteness of the subaltern' and the 'unthought limit of western epistemology' (Varadharajan 1995: 94). In Varadharajan's argument, Adorno's approach differs significantly from that of Derrida because 'it seeks to redeem the object in its alterity' (Varadharajan 1995: 79).

Varadharajan's distinction between the concrete, material lives of the oppressed and the limits of western knowledge is illuminating, but the conclusion drawn from this distinction crucially ignores the similarities between the ethical dimensions of Derrida's deconstruction and Adorno's critical philosophy. By doing so, Varadharajan misses the point that the deconstructive emphasis on complicity also contains an important ethical agenda. For Spivak's affirmation of complicity does not simply paralyse or derail the practice of critical or political thinking from the start. Rather, Spivak's acknowledgement of complicity provides a crucial starting point from which to develop a more responsible intellectual practice.

In a commentary on Spivak's thought, Robert Young (1990) similarly misreads this ethical rethinking of politics as a sign of Spivak's 'residual classical Marxism [which] is invoked for the force of its political effects from an outside that disavows and apparently escapes the strictures that the rest of her work establishes' (Young 1990: 173). There is certainly a move in Spivak's work to interrupt the narrow, disciplinary framework of deconstruction through an ethical engagement with specific political concerns. In 'Responsibility' (1994), for example, Spivak interrupts a meticulous discussion of Derrida's analysis of Martin Heidegger's philosophy to discuss the limitations of the World Bank's 1993 Flood Action Plan in Bangladesh. And in 'The Setting to Work of Deconstruction' (1999) Spivak interrupts a summary of Jacques Derrida's thought with an analysis of counter-globalist development activism.

Such a mode of writing clearly breaks with the strict disciplinary codes and conventions of western critical theory. Yet to frame this break in the classic materialist terms of a rigid division between theory and practice ignores how Spivak has reworked the ethical dimensions of critical theory (especially deconstruction), as well as the theoretical assumptions informing political practice.

ETHICS, POLITICS AND 'THE SETTING TO WORK OF DECONSTRUCTION'

In 'The Setting to Work of Deconstruction' (1999), Spivak brilliantly elaborates the ethical-political position of her own work through a careful survey of Jacques Derrida's thought. Starting with a discussion of key European philosophical influences in Derrida's early work, Spivak traces a gradual move in Derrida's work from the conceptual limits of western philosophical discourse to 'a greater emphasis on ethics and its relationship to the political' (Spivak 1999: 426).

Spivak refers to Derrida's engagement with Levinas and the ethical encounter with the Other as affirmative deconstruction because it embraces or 'affirms' the inevitable risk of falling prey in a certain way to the old structure that it seeks to criticise. At the same time, this affirmation of falling prey is performed in the hope that the old structure will eventually be altered by the Other at some indeterminate point in the future. This deconstruction of ethics is painstaking because it takes a long time to think and to explain. What is more, there are no guarantees that the careful thought and articulation of deconstruction will make any difference in real, political terms.

Despite these difficulties, Spivak has productively engaged with Derrida's discussions of ethical themes such as responsibility, friendship, internationalism and democracy, and reworked them in the field of 'Third World' counter-globalist development activism. In the 'Translator's Preface' to *Imaginary Maps*, a collection of short stories by Mahasweta Devi, Spivak describes the 'painstaking labour' required 'to establish ethical singularity with the subaltern' (Devi 1995: xxv). The paradox of this singular ethical relationship is that there is no prior example that can demonstrate this ethical approach; it depends on the context. Indeed, Spivak characterises this ethical rapport as an 'experience of the impossible' because it is impossible to engage with every oppressed person in the same way. Nevertheless, Spivak does find an allegory of this ethical relation in 'Pterodactyl, Pirtha and Puran Sahay', a short story by Mahasweta Devi. In a sequence where the fictional protagonist, Puran (a benevolent, middle-class journalist), sees a cave drawing of a pterodactyl drawn by a lower caste tribal boy, Spivak argues that 'Puran becomes part of the tribe's ongoing historical record' (Spivak 1995b: 256). For Spivak, this event in the text approximates an ethical response because Puran recognises the singular condition of rural tribal societies in India, and how 'the alibis of Development [are used] to exploit the tribals and destroy their life-system' (Spivak 1995b: 256).

More recently, in 'A Note on the New International' (2001) Spivak has described her own long-term involvement in teacher training programmes to encourage literacy for poor, underprivileged children in rural schools based in India and Bangladesh. Echoing Derrida 'on another register', Spivak emphasises that 'real, mind-changing formations of collectivity, that will withstand and survive victory, is incredibly slow and time-consuming work, with no guarantees' (Spivak 2001: 15). Invoking Derrida's 'plea for slow reading, even at a time of political urgency', Spivak makes a similar 'plea for the patient work of learning to learn from' the oppressed rather than speaking for them (15).

In *The Ethics of Deconstruction*, Simon Critchley identifies an impasse in deconstruction, where Derrida's interminable tracing of the undecidability that structures all political decision-making actually prevents the 'passage from undecidability to the decision' or 'from ethics to politics' (Critchley 1992: 236–7). For Critchley, deconstruction is in danger of becoming a formal abstraction that is empty of any determinate political content (237). Spivak's emphasis on the setting to work of deconstruction may appear to repeat this formal abstraction to the extent that it is consistent with Derrida's turn towards affirmative deconstruction. But what crucially distinguishes Spivak's employment of affirmative deconstruction from the work of Derrida is the way that Spivak also interrupts the strict theoretical and philosophical terms of Derrida's argument with 'political' examples from the histories of subaltern agency and resistance in the 'Third World'. In 'Strategy, Identity, Writing' (1990), for example, Spivak emphasises how this affirmative mode of deconstruction obliges you to 'say yes to that which interrupts your project', to the 'political' that interrupts 'theory' (Spivak 1990: 47). Derrida emphasises the madness of undecidability that necessarily structures all political decision-making, but he never actually makes any political decisions in his writing. By contrast, Spivak grounds the slow and painstaking movement from ethics to politics in the concrete, everyday struggles of subaltern communities to become literate, political citizens in their own terms.

SUMMARY

Spivak's thought has been profoundly shaped by the critical strategies of deconstruction, as well as making the early work of Jacques Derrida accessible to the English-speaking world. Spivak's use of deconstruction has often been invoked to demonstrate a perceived contradiction between Spivak's 'materialist commitment' to engage with disenfranchised, subaltern groups in the 'Third World', and the difficult theoretical language and methodologies she employs to achieve this goal. Yet, such critiques tend to overlook the following important points:

- the influence of Derrida's deconstruction of western philosophical truth and the western humanist subject on the development of Spivak's postcolonial thought;
- the ethical dimensions of deconstruction and the relevance of the ethical turn in deconstruction to Spivak's postcolonial reading practices and counter-global development activism;
- the imperative to move from ethics to politics, and to set deconstruction to work outside the academic disciplinary framework of literary criticism and philosophy in a wider field of global economic and political relations.

LEARNING FROM
THE SUBALTERN

One of the most important and complex aspects of Spivak's thought is her ongoing attempt to find a critical vocabulary that is appropriate to describe the experiences and histories of particular individuals and social groups, who have been historically dispossessed and exploited by European colonialism. In the context of political struggles for national independence or anti-colonial resistance, the use of master words like 'the colonised', 'woman' or 'the worker' may seem to provide a coherent political identity for disempowered individuals and groups to unite against a common oppressor.

As we saw in the previous chapter, however, for Spivak these master words do not do justice to the lives and histories of those people who were frequently ignored and subsequently forgotten by anti-colonial national independence movements. In the place of these political master words, Spivak proposes the word subaltern to encompass a range of different subject positions which are not predefined by dominant political discourses.

For Spivak the term 'subaltern' is useful because it is flexible; it can accommodate social identities and struggles (such as woman and the colonised) that do not fall under the reductive terms of 'strict class-analysis'. As she asserts in an interview published in the US journal *Polygraph*:

I like the word 'subaltern' for one reason. It is truly situational. 'Subaltern' began as a description of a certain rank in the military. The word was used under censorship by Gramsci: he called Marxism 'monism,' and was obliged to call the proletarian 'subaltern.' That word, used under duress, has been transformed into the description of everything that doesn't fall under strict class analysis. I like that, because it has no theoretical rigor.

(Spivak 1990: 141)

In response to Spivak's definition, the first section of this chapter will trace the intellectual and theoretical sources that have influenced Spivak's discussions of the subaltern. This will be followed by a consideration of Spivak's reading of a group of historians known as the Subaltern Studies collective and an examination of her critique of political representation. Finally, the chapter examines what is at stake in Spivak's provocative (and frequently misunderstood) assertion that the subaltern cannot speak.

THE POSTCOLONIAL INTELLECTUAL AND POLITICAL RESPONSIBILITY

The brutal economic exploitation and political oppression of disempowered, subaltern groups in the postcolonial world presents an ethical dilemma as well as a methodological challenge to Spivak, as a public intellectual who is committed to articulating the lives and histories of such groups in an appropriate and non-exploitative way.

Indeed, as Spivak's writing demonstrates, the experience of social and political oppression in postcolonial societies such as India cuts across differences in class, region, language, ethnicity, religion, generation, gender and citizenship. Because of these differences, there is a risk that any general claims or theoretical statements made on behalf of disempowered subaltern populations by educated, metropolitan-based intellectuals will overlook crucial social differences between particular subaltern groups.

Furthermore, in the context of the western academy, there is a risk that western-educated postcolonial intellectuals such as Spivak will be perceived by their western readership as speaking for the disempowered.

As suggested in Chapter 2, Spivak's engagement with the historical knowledge and experience of disempowered groups is persistently critical of any attempt (including her own) to fully explain and know the experiences of the disempowered, as an object of thought. Part of this critical endeavour reflects a 'vigilance to errors committed exploitatively against the disenfranchised' (Chow 1998: 40). Indeed, for Spivak, the singularity of each of the disempowered people she engages with tests the limits of dominant narratives of social change and political representation.

We have already seen, for example, Spivak's criticism of the emancipatory promises of bourgeois nationalism in India, through her reading of Mahasweta Devi's short story 'Breast Giver'. For Spivak, the gradual decay and disease of Jashoda's exploited maternal body challenges the bourgeois nationalist myth of Mother India from the standpoint of a subaltern woman. As I go on to suggest later in the book, Spivak's translation and textual commentaries on the fiction of Mahasweta Devi provide a powerful counterpoint to the erasure of women, peasants and the tribals from the dominant historical and political discourses of India. Yet this erasure is also importantly highlighted in Spivak's critical engagement with the Subaltern Studies collective, a group of educated, Marxist historians based in India, Britain and the USA, who are concerned to retrieve the history of peasant insurgency before, during and after British colonial rule in India (1857–1947). Spivak's engagement with the Subaltern Studies historians highlights the political achievements of the collective in their ongoing attempt to recover the histories of peasant insurgency and resistance before and after India's independence from the British. Yet Spivak also emphasises that the classic Marxist methodology of the Subaltern Studies collective prevents them from reading the histories of women's resistance in India.

THE SUBALTERN

Before looking at Spivak's critique of the Subaltern Studies collective, and her own examples of subalternity in more detail, it is important to situate the historical and cultural meanings of the term subaltern.

Antonio Gramsci's account of the subaltern provides a key theoretical resource for understanding the conditions of the poor, the lower class and peasantry in India partly because of the parallels he drew between the division of labour in Mussolini's Italy and the colonial division of labour in India. What is more, Gramsci emphasised that the oppression of the rural peasantry in Southern Italy could be subverted

SUBALTERN

Although the term subaltern conventionally denotes a junior ranking officer in the British army (*OED*), the most significant intellectual sources for Spivak's definition of the subaltern are the early twentieth-century Italian Marxist thinker Antonio Gramsci (1891–1937) and the work of the mainly Indian-based Subaltern Studies collective. In the *Prison Notebooks*, written during the time of Mussolini's fascist government in Italy, Gramsci used the term subaltern interchangeably with '"subordinate" [. . .] or sometimes "instrumental" to denote "[n]on hegemonic groups or classes"' (Gramsci 1978: xiv). Gramsci used the term subaltern to refer in particular to the un-organised groups of rural peasants based in Southern Italy, who had no social or political consciousness as a group, and were therefore suscep-tible to the ruling ideas, culture and leadership of the state. Gramsci's account of the subaltern has been further developed by a group of historians known as the Subaltern Studies collective. Extending the terms of Gramsci's original definition, these historians define subaltern as 'the general attribute of subordination in South Asian society, whether this is expressed in terms of class, caste, age, gender and office or in any other way' (Guha 1988: 35). For the Subaltern Studies historians, Gramsci's discussion of the oppression of the rural peasantry in Southern Italy aptly described the continued oppression of the rural peasantry, the working class, and the untouchables in post-independence Indian society. Indeed, the problem for the Subaltern Studies historians was that India had achieved political independence from the British Empire without the corresponding social revolution in the class system it had originally hoped for. Spivak generally agrees with the histori-cal arguments of the Subaltern Studies collective, but adds that their lin-gering classic Marxist approach to social and historical change effectively privileges the male subaltern subject as the primary agent of change. This is problematic for two reasons. First, the classic Marxist model overlooks the lives and struggles of women, before, during and after India's indepen-dence. And second, the Marxist model of historical change, which anti-colo-nial nationalist leaders had originally invoked to try to mobilise the subaltern, had clearly failed in the end to change the subaltern's social and economic circumstances. In the place of this classic Marxist definition, Spivak pro-poses a more nuanced, flexible, post-Marxist definition of the subaltern, informed by deconstruction, which takes women's lives and histories into account.

through an alliance with the urban working class, or through the development of class-consciousness among the peasants. To this extent, Gramsci's account of the subaltern resembled Karl Marx's earlier proclamation in the nineteenth century that the industrial working class in Europe carried the future potential for collective social and political change. Unlike Marx's model of social and political change, however, Gramsci stressed that the social and political practices of the rural peasantry were not systematic or coherent in their opposition to the state. It is this lack of coherence that distinguishes Gramsci's notion of the subaltern from the traditional Marxist perception of the industrial working class as unified and coherent. Furthermore, this lack of a coherent political identity in Gramsci's description of the subaltern is also crucial to Spivak's discussion of the subaltern in the postcolonial world.

DECONSTRUCTING HISTORIOGRAPHY: SPIVAK'S CRITIQUE OF THE SUBALTERN STUDIES COLLECTIVE

As I have already suggested, the meaning of the term subaltern is broad and encompasses a range of different social locations. In the social context of India's rigid class and caste system, the location of the subaltern is further effaced by the layered histories of European colonialism and national independence. In response to these changing historical conditions, Spivak has, from the beginning, sought to find an appropriate methodology for articulating the histories and struggles of disempowered groups.

If Antonio Gramsci's account of the rural peasantry in Italian history provides a key theoretical resource for Spivak's ongoing discussions of subalternity, one of the most important historical resources comes from the discussions of peasant insurgency and resistance movements in India by the Subaltern Studies historians, including Shahid Amin (1950–), David Arnold (1946–), Partha Chatterjee (1947–), David Hardiman (1947–), Ranajit Guha (1923–), and Gyanendra Pandey (1950–). In a multi-volume series of collected essays entitled *Subaltern Studies* these historians have consistently attempted to recover a history of subaltern agency and resistance from the perspective of the people, rather than that of the state.

Traditionally, the histories of the rural peasantry and the urban working class had been recorded by elite social groups. At first, these subaltern histories were documented in the archives of British colonial administrators; they were then later rewritten in the historical reports of the educated Indian, middle-class elite, during and after the struggle for national independence. As Ranajit Guha asserts in 'On Some Aspects of the Historiography of Colonial India':

> The historiography of Indian nationalism has for a long time been dominated by elitism and bourgeois nationalist elitism. Both originated as the ideological product of British rule in India, but have survived the transfer of power and have been assimilated to neo-colonialist and neo-nationalist forms of discourse in Britain and India respectively.
>
> (Guha 1988: 37)

The historical representation of the various lower-class subaltern groups was thus framed in the terms and interests of the ruling power, or dominant social class. In the historical archives of the British Empire, the lives and political agencies of the rural peasantry in India were subordinated to the larger project of imperial governance and social control; in the elite narratives of bourgeois national independence, the localised resistance movements of the peasants were subordinated to the larger nationalist project of decolonisation. In both cases, the complex social and political histories of particular subaltern groups were not recognised or represented.

The success of a rural peasant rebellion against the Indian national government in the Naxalbari area of West Bengal in 1967 prompted the Subaltern Studies historians to rethink the national independence narrative from the perspective of the subaltern. This in turn led the historians to reconstruct the various histories of subaltern insurgency, which were autonomous of and separate from the mainstream, bourgeois nationalist independence movement. This has not been an easy task. For the Subaltern Studies historians, the attempt to recover these histories of autonomous resistance and struggle was hampered by the lack of any reliable historical sources or documents reflecting the social conditions and practices of subaltern groups *in their own terms*.

The political voice and agency of particular subaltern groups was often indistinguishable from the elite characterisation of peasant movements as spontaneous acts of violence, with no political content or organisation. Faced with this absence of reliable historical material, the Subaltern Studies historians attempted to recuperate the political voice, will and agency of the subaltern through a critique of colonial and elite historical representation.

It is this approach to dominant historical writing or historiography in the work of the Subaltern Studies historians that is crucial to Spivak's early theoretical discussions of the subaltern in the late 1980s. For Spivak, the critique of elite historical representation has a clear and distinct political agenda. If the subaltern's political voice and agency could not be *retrieved* from the archive of colonial or elite nationalist histories, then it could perhaps be gradually *re-inscribed* through a critique of dominant historical representation.

In her discussion of the Subaltern Studies project, Spivak initially contends that a classic Marxist notion of history informs the theoretical approach of the group to the histories of subaltern insurgency and protest in India. As Spivak writes:

> The work of the Subaltern Studies group offers a theory of change. The insertion of India into colonialism is generally defined as a change from semi-feudalism into capitalist subjection. Such a definition theorizes the change within the great narrative of the modes of production, and by uneasy implication, within the narrative of the transition from feudalism to capitalism.
>
> (Spivak 1987: 197)

In common with other Subaltern Studies historians, Spivak's discussion emphasises how the histories of peasant uprisings and social action present a crisis in the historical narrative of Indian national independence. Yet Spivak also questions whether the Marxist methodology informing the approach of the Subaltern Studies historians is appropriate to describe the complex history of subaltern insurgency.

It is important to remember that Spivak's thought does not take place in a historical or intellectual vacuum. As Robert Young (2001) emphasises in a rigorous cultural history of Indian postcolonial thought, Marxism had played a central role in the evolution of Indian political thought since the early twentieth century (Young 2001: 312). M.N. Roy, the leading figure in early twentieth-century Indian communism, had famously disagreed 'with Lenin on the latter's idea that parties of the proletariat should support bourgeois national liberation movements' (Young 2001: 312). As Young goes on to point out, the subsequent refusal of the Indian Communist Party to 'put the colonial conflict above that of internal class conflict' (315) caused it to lose political support to the Congress Party, which prioritised national liberation over the class struggle. Yet, despite this electoral defeat of the Indian communist party, Marxism continued to influence political thinking in India, both in the 1967 Naxalbari peasant rebellion against the Congress Party, and in the subsequent historical research of the Subaltern Studies collective.

By situating Spivak's critique of the Marxist methodology that informs the Subaltern Studies research in the context of these earlier political debates, one can see that Spivak is not simply rejecting Marxist thought altogether. As Robert Young emphasises, Spivak's thought revises and adapts the categories of Marxist thought beyond the narrow terms of class politics to include other forms of liberation struggles, such as the women's movement, the peasant struggles or the rights of indigenous minorities (Young 2001: 351). Indeed, one of the main reasons that Spivak criticises the employment of a *classic* Marxist methodology in the work of the Subaltern Studies historians is because it is too rigid to describe the complexities of Indian social history.

In Karl Marx's analysis of capitalism in nineteenth-century Europe, the transformation in economic and social relations between the property-owning classes (or the bourgeoisie) and the working class (or the proletariat) formed the basis for his model of social and historical change. As Spivak points out, however, this historical shift from feudalism to capitalism in India may offer a historical account of how middle-class colonised subjects became national subjects after colonialism, but it does not account for the lives and struggles of other disempowered groups, including peasants, women and indigenous groups.

Against the Marxist approach of the Subaltern historians, Spivak reads the historical research of the Subaltern Studies collective as tracing a series of political 'confrontations' between dominant and exploited groups rather than simply noting the transition from 'semi-feudalism into capitalist subjection' (Spivak 1987: 197). Such confrontations may not have any direct political or economic impact on the state, but this does not mean that they are devoid of political agency or meaning.

By shifting the critical perspective from India's national liberation movement to a focus on the social movements and agency of particular disempowered, subaltern groups, Spivak encourages us to consider how 'the agency of change is located in the insurgent or "subaltern"' (Spivak 1987: 197). Such a shift in perspective also necessitates a parallel shift in the methodology informing that perspective.

SUBALTERN STUDIES AND THE QUESTION OF METHODOLOGY

Spivak's reading of the Subaltern Studies historians' project emphasises how their practice of revisionist historical writing is broadly speaking at odds with their methodology. Early writings on the history of peasant insurgency, such as Ranajit Guha's *Elementary Aspects of Peasant Insurgency* (1983), try to recover a pure subaltern consciousness that is equivalent to Marx's notion of class consciousness. Spivak argues that such an approach bestows a false coherence on to the much more complex and differentiated struggles of particular subaltern groups. By doing so, the Subaltern Studies historians are in danger of objectifying the subaltern, and thereby controlling 'through knowledge even as they restore versions of causality and self determination to him' (Spivak 1988: 201).

Rather than disavowing this risk of falling prey to the dominant structures of knowledge and representation, Spivak emphasises that this risk is necessary in order to address the subaltern voices and histories they are studying. In this particular context, Spivak invokes Derrida's statement (discussed in more detail in Chapter 2) that 'the enterprise of deconstruction always in a certain way falls prey to its own work' (cited in Spivak 1987: 201). By affirming the risk of complicity in the Subaltern Studies work (rather than disavowing it), Spivak suggests that the 'actual practice' of the Subaltern Studies historians is 'closer to deconstruction' (Spivak 1987: 198).

Spivak's deconstructive reading of the Subaltern Studies historians 'against the grain' of their avowedly Marxist methodology has generated much controversy. The main reason for this is that Spivak is seen to impose yet another elite western academic language on to the history of subaltern insurgency. Rosalind O'Hanlon, for instance, argues that 'those who set out to restore' the 'presence' of the subaltern 'end only by borrowing the tools of that discourse, tools which serve only to re-duplicate the first subjection which they effect, in the realms of critical theory' (O'Hanlon 1988: 218).

Yet Spivak is not simply opposing deconstruction and Marxism. What Spivak crucially objects to in the early research of the Subaltern Studies historians is the idea that the subaltern is a sovereign political subject in control of her own destiny. Spivak vehemently opposes this idea on the grounds that the sovereign subaltern subject is an effect of the dominant discourse of the elite. (For more on discourse, see box,

p. 85.) As Spivak asserts, 'the texts of counter-insurgency locate [. . .] a will as a sovereign cause when it is no more than an effect of the sub-altern subject effect' (Spivak 1988: 204). In Spivak's view, the political will of the subaltern is constructed by the dominant discourse as an after effect of elite nationalism. This discourse contains the subaltern within the grand narrative of bourgeois national liberation, and totally ignores the different, local struggles of particular subaltern groups, such as the role of Muslim weavers in Northern India during the 1857 Indian mutiny; the industrial action of Jute workers in early twentieth-century Calcutta; or the Awadh peasant rebellion of 1920.

From one point of view, it might appear that Spivak's claim that the subaltern subject is a discursive effect removes the very ground for effective political struggle. Indeed, the postcolonial literary critic Neil Lazarus has argued that Spivak is not really concerned with 'native agency at all, but a theory of the way in which the social and symbolic practice of the disenfranchised elements of the native population are *represented* (or more accurately, *not represented*) in colonialist-elitist discourse' (Lazarus 1999: 112).

Lazarus's comments are illuminating here, but they ignore how the charting of a subaltern subject effect is only the first step in Spivak's deconstructive reading of Indian society. By emphasising how the sub-altern subject is constructed through the dominant discourse of elite nationalism, Spivak also defines the particular struggles of women, peas-ants and the tribals as separate from and supplementary to the dominant historical narrative of bourgeois national independence.

Against the claims of the elite group to represent the nation as a coherent, objective structure, Spivak further emphasises that Indian society, the terrain of social struggle, is 'a continuous sign chain' or a network of traces (Spivak 1987: 198). This use of a deconstructive vocabulary provides Spivak with a more flexible methodology to describe the histories and struggles of disenfranchised subaltern groups, such as peasants, women and the tribals who are not accounted for in the classic Marxist terms of the class struggle. In this more flexible, post-Marxist deconstructive account of political struggle, 'the possibility of action lies in the dynamics of the disruption of this object [the social], the breaking and relinking of the chain' (Spivak 1987: 198).

Spivak's careful deconstructive reading of subaltern insurgency often frustrates readers seeking a clear political solution to the plight of oppressed groups. Neil Lazarus, for example, bemoans the fact that 'an investigation of the history of "Third World Women" is typically deferred in [Spivak's] writing' (Lazarus 1999: 113). At times Spivak's deconstructive strategies of reading the histories of subaltern insurgency may certainly appear to suspend the elaboration of a concrete example of political resistance.

Yet this is not to say that considerations of subaltern insurgency and resistance are entirely absent from Spivak's thought. Indeed, Spivak's clearest investigations of 'Third World', subaltern women's resistance are often seen in her engagements with literary texts. In 'A Literary Representation of the Subaltern', Spivak suggests that literary texts can provide an alternative rhetorical site for articulating the histories of subaltern women. Invoking the fiction of Mahasweta Devi, Spivak emphasises that Devi frequently bases her stories on events in twentieth-century Indian history. In 'Draupadi', for example, Devi charts the struggle, eventual capture and brutal rape of a female revolutionary, Dopdi Mejhen, who is wanted by the military for her involvement in the Naxalite rebellion against the bourgeois, nationalist government and the landowners in the 1960s and 1970s. For Spivak, Dopdi's final moment of resistance, when she stands naked and defiant against the military commander, Senanayak, provides an 'allegory of the woman's struggle within the revolution in a shifting historical moment' (Spivak 1987: 184).

The political significance of Devi's fiction and its impact on Spivak's thought is examined more closely in Chapter 6. Nonetheless, it is important to remember that Spivak's readings of Devi's female subaltern characters provide an important counterpoint to the silencing and erasure of women in the British colonial archives and elite nationalist historical writing in India. Since official historical discourse tends to privilege men as the main actors of revolutionary politics in India, Spivak suggests that literature can provide a different space to articulate subaltern women's insurgency and resistance in the social text of postcolonial India. More specifically, the historical fiction of Mahasweta Devi provides Spivak with a concrete articulation of subaltern women's agency and resistance in the postcolonial world.

Spivak's approach to the history of subaltern insurgency through the careful critical strategies of deconstruction may appear to reduce the lives and struggles of subaltern groups to 'the pages of a book' (Spivak 1987: 198). Yet, Spivak's analysis of the social text importantly recalls Jacques Derrida's discussion of general writing in *Of Grammatology*.

In Derrida's argument, general writing refers not only to printed matter on a page, but to any text – visual, vocal, cinematic, historical, social or political – which is made meaningful by a system of signs or codes.

By emphasising how intellectuals are a part of the larger social text that they describe, Spivak resists the 'desire to find a [subaltern] consciousness [. . .] in a positive and pure state' (Spivak 1987: 198). Indeed, for Spivak, such a model of political consciousness and subjectivity (which is prevalent in the Marxist vocabulary of the Subaltern Studies historians) paradoxically works to '"objectify" the subaltern' and 'control him through knowledge even as they restore versions of causality and self-determination to him' (Spivak 1987: 201).

Instead, Spivak approaches the history of subaltern insurgency as 'a functional change in a sign system' (Spivak 1987: 201), an approach that expands and deepens the Marxist approach of the subaltern historians to include women, as well as the rural peasantry and the urban proletariat. Furthermore, by deconstructing the political claims made by the Subaltern Studies historians, Spivak patiently attempts to transform conditions of impossibility – the hopeless and negative feeling that nothing will change for the disenfranchised – into a condition of possibility.

CAN THE SUBALTERN SPEAK?

Spivak's critique of western models of class-consciousness and subjectivity is further developed in 'Can the Subaltern Speak?', an essay that was first published in the journal *Wedge* (1985) and later reprinted in a collection of essays, entitled *Marxism and the Interpretation of Culture* (1988). In this essay, Spivak juxtaposes the radical claims of twentieth-century French intellectuals such as Michel Foucault and Gilles Deleuze to speak for the disenfranchised and the self-righteous claims of British colonialism to rescue native women from the practice of Hindu widow sacrifice in nineteenth-century India. The point of this juxtaposition is to emphasise how the benevolent, radical western intellectual can paradoxically silence the subaltern by claiming to represent and speak for their experience, in the same way that the benevolent colonialist silenced the voice of the widow, who 'chooses' to die on her husband's funeral pyre. As I go on to suggest, in both of these examples, the benevolent impulse to represent subaltern groups effectively appropriates the voice of the subaltern and thereby silences them.

Political representation may seem like an obvious goal for subaltern groups to escape from exploitation. Yet, as 'Can the Subaltern Speak?' reveals, the historical and structural conditions of political representation do not guarantee that the interests of particular subaltern groups will be recognised or that their voices will be heard.

Spivak's critique of Deleuze and Foucault starts from her premise that the structures underpinning aesthetic representation (in artistic, literary or cinematic texts) also underpin political representation. The general difference between aesthetic and political structures of representation is that aesthetic representation tends to foreground its status as a re-presentation of the real, whereas political representation denies this structure of representation.

For Spivak, the problem with Foucault and Deleuze is that they efface their role as intellectuals in representing the disempowered groups they describe. Spivak compares this effacement to a masquerade in which the intellectual as an 'absent nonrepresenter [. . .] lets the oppressed speak for themselves' (Spivak 1988: 292). Despite all the intellectual energy Foucault and Deleuze invest in showing how subjects are constructed through discourse and representation (see Chapter 3), Spivak argues that when it comes to discussing real, historical examples of social and political struggle, Foucault and Deleuze fall back on a transparent model of representation, in which 'oppressed subjects speak, act and know' their own conditions (Spivak 1988: 276).

Surprisingly, Spivak goes on to clarify this criticism through a discussion of political representation in Karl Marx's *Eighteenth Brumaire of Louis Bonaparte* (1852). This move is particularly unexpected because it seems to show that Marx does take issues of textuality seriously.

In *The Eighteenth Brumaire of Louis Bonaparte*, Marx offers a description of small, peasant proprietors in nineteenth-century French agrarian society. For Marx, these people do not collectively represent a coherent class; indeed, their conditions of economic and social life prevent them from having class-consciousness. For this reason, the '(absent collective) consciousness of the small peasant proprietor' (Spivak 1988: 276) is symbolically depicted by a political representative or proxy from the middle class, who speaks on their behalf.

For Marx, the representation of the peasant proprietors has a double meaning, which is distinguished in the German by the terms *darstellen* (representation as aesthetic portrait) and *vertreten* (representation by political proxy) (Spivak 1988: 276–9). In the Foucault–Deleuze conversation, Spivak argues that these two meanings of representation are conflated; for in the constitution of disempowered groups as coherent political subjects, the process of (aesthetic) representation is subordinated to the voice of the political proxy who speaks on their behalf. As a consequence of this conflation, the aesthetic portrait – symbolically representing disempowered people as coherent political subjects – is often taken as a transparent expression of their political desire and interests.

More importantly, Spivak argues that this act of rhetorical conflation can have potentially injurious effects on the oppressed groups that certain left-wing intellectuals claim to speak for. In the case of Foucault and Deleuze, these groups include factory workers and people who are incarcerated in prisons or psychiatric institutions in the west.

When this model of political representation is mapped on to the 'Third World', the gap between aesthetic and political representation is even more pronounced. For Spivak, this gap is exemplified by western feminism's tendency to speak on behalf of 'Third World' women. (This particular power relationship will be dealt with more fully in Chapter 4.) Noting the impossibility of an equal alliance-based politics between western feminist intellectuals and 'Third World' women, Spivak asserts that:

> On the other side of the international division of labour, the subject of exploitation cannot know and speak the text of female exploitation even if the absurdity of the nonrepresenting intellectual making space for her to speak is achieved.
>
> (Spivak 1988: 289)

Spivak's ongoing discussions of disempowered subaltern women serve to highlight the limitations of applying European theories of representation to the lives and histories of disempowered women in the 'Third World'. Unless western intellectuals begin to take the aesthetic dimension of political representation into account, Spivak argues that these intellectuals will continue to silence the voice of subaltern women.

'Can the Subaltern Speak?' has been read as illustrating Spivak's own position as a postcolonial intellectual, who is concerned to excavate the disempowered and silenced voices of the past from the material and political context of the present. Unlike Spivak's reading of the Subaltern Studies historical work, this essay combines Spivak's political re-formulation of western poststructuralist methodologies with a re-

reading of the nineteenth-century colonial archives in India. What is more, the essay signals a departure from the historical work of the Subaltern Studies group in that Spivak focuses on the historical experiences of subaltern women, a constituency whose voices and social locations have generally been ignored by the Subaltern Studies collective, as well as by colonial and elite historical scholarship.

By engaging with the historical knowledge of such disempowered women, Spivak expands the original definition of the subaltern, developed by Ranajit Guha and others, to include the struggles and experiences of women. This expansion of the term subaltern further complicates the lower-class connotations of the word because it includes women from the upper middle class, as well as the peasantry and the sub-proletariat.

Nevertheless, the crucial point for Spivak is that the active involvement of women in the history of anti-British-colonial insurgency in India has been excluded from the official history of national independence. As Spivak writes:

> Within the effaced itinerary of the subaltern subject, the track of sexual difference is doubly effaced. The question is not of female participation in insurgency, or the ground rules of the sexual division of labour, for both of which there is 'evidence'. It is, rather, that, both as object of colonialist historiography and as subject of insurgency, the ideological construction of gender keeps the male dominant. If, in the context of colonial production, the subaltern has no history and cannot speak, the subaltern as female is even more deeply in shadow.
>
> (Spivak 1988: 287)

This emphasis on the gendered location of subaltern women expands and complicates the established concept of the subaltern, as outlined above. Yet as Neil Lazarus emphasises, Spivak's injunction to investigate the histories of subaltern women's insurgency is rarely accompanied by any substantial historical research (Lazarus 1999: 113). The reason for this, as Spivak points out, is because 'the ideological construction of gender' in the colonial archives and the historical records of subaltern insurgency 'keeps the male dominant' (Spivak 1988: 281). Against this historical erasure of subaltern women, Spivak thus traces the disappearance of the subaltern woman in order to articulate their material and cultural histories.

RECOVERING WOMEN'S HISTORIES IN THE COLONIAL ARCHIVES

The focus on disempowered women as subaltern subjects in Spivak's work may seem to dislodge the articulation of subaltern histories from their particular class-based formations. However, Spivak is not simply substituting a gendered notion of the subaltern for a class-based notion. Spivak rather emphasises how an exclusive focus on class and economic location overlooks the material practices and historical role of women in the transition from colonialism to national independence in India (1757–1947).

In 'The Rani of Sirmur' (1985a), for example, Spivak explicitly addresses how a high-caste woman was written into and out of the colonial archives, during a period in the 1840s when India was passing from the deregulated economic control of the East India Company to direct colonial rule by the British government. As Spivak notes, '[The Rani of Sirmur] emerges in the colonial archives because of the commercial/territorial interests of the East India Company' (Spivak 1985a: 263).

The state of Sirmur was located in the hills of Northern India, an area of strategic political and economic interest to the East India Company. At the time, '[t]he entire eastern half of Sirmur had to be annexed immediately, and all of it eventually, to secure the company's trade routes and frontier against Nepal' (Spivak 1985a: 266). To execute this task, the British had deposed the Raja of Sirmur, Karma Prakash, on the grounds that 'he was barbaric and dissolute' (Spivak 1985a: 265). In his place, '[t]he Rani is established as the immediate guardian of the minor king Fatteh Prakash, her son, because there are no trustworthy male relatives in the royal house' (Spivak 1985a: 265). The reason that the Rani is installed on the throne, Spivak contends, is 'because she is a king's wife and a weaker vessel' (Spivak 1985a: 266). At this particular historical moment in India, the Rani's privileged social and economic position is thus subordinated to her gendered identity as a mother of the future King and as a widow to the Raja.

For the British colonial administrators in India at the time, there was a perceived conflict between the Rani's two roles as widow and mother. As Spivak emphasises, the British colonial archives reveal an implicit anxiety that the Rani would perform the ritual of *Sati* (widow-sacrifice) on her deceased husband's funeral pyre, leaving the heir to the throne without a guardian, and the state without a leader (who could be easily influenced by the British). When the Rani is no longer useful to the economic interests of the East India Company, or the political interest of the emerging British colonial government, she disappears from the archives. These particular historical conditions lead Spivak to conclude that, 'The Rani emerges only when she is needed in the space of imperial production' (Spivak 1985a: 270).

'The Rani of Sirmur' reveals two important points about Spivak's discussions of the subaltern woman. First, the essay shows how Spivak's analysis of the colonial archives differs from the colonial discourse analysis of Edward Said and Homi Bhabha by focusing specifically on the plight of 'Third World' women. In this respect, Spivak challenges the gender blindness of earlier postcolonial theories from a feminist standpoint. Second, the essay demonstrates how Spivak's expanded definition of the term subaltern to include women complicates the narrow, class-based definition of the term.

This expanded definition has enabled critics such as Gita Rajan to claim that the former Indian Prime Minister, Indira Gandhi, was a subaltern subject because she manipulated her status as a woman, a mother and a widow in order to gain political support from the elder male members of the Congress Party, as well as the people. Rajan's discussion of Indira Gandhi as a subaltern subject illustrates one of the difficulties with Spivak's flexible use of the term to describe upper-middle-class elite women as well as disenfranchised women. Indeed, some of Spivak's critics have argued that the term subaltern is used inconsistently to denote a broad range of disempowered social groups and positions, including upper-middle-class women such as the Rani of Sirmur, as well as subsistence farmers, unorganised peasant movements, tribal groups and the urban sub-proletariat. Bart Moore-Gilbert, for example, contends that:

> Spivak extends the reach of the term [subaltern] in essays like 'Can the Subaltern Speak?' by using it to figure social groups 'further down' the social scale and consequently even less visible to colonial and Third World national-bourgeois historiography alike; she is especially preoccupied by 'subsistence farmers, unorganised peasant labour, the tribals and communities of zero workers on the street or in the countryside'. More particularly, her analysis is directed at the subject-position of the female subaltern, whom she describes as doubly marginalized by virtue of relative economic disadvantage and gender subordination.
>
> (Moore-Gilbert 1997: 80)

For Spivak, however, this is precisely the point. The expansion of the category of subaltern to include women emphasises how the subaltern is not only subject to a rigid class system, but also to the patriarchal discourses of religion, the family and the colonial state. Indeed, this is borne out in Spivak's detailed discussion of the representation of widow sacrifice in the second half of 'Can the Subaltern Speak?'.

SATI AND THE LIMITS OF REPRESENTATION

Spivak's discussion of widow self-immolation or *sati* in 'The Rani of Sirmur' is developed further in 'Can the Subaltern Speak?'. Citing ancient archival sources from Hindu and Vedic religious texts and the legislative discourses of the British Empire, Spivak initially considers how the political will and voice of Hindu women are represented in accounts of widow self-immolation.

In the terms of ancient Hindu religious texts such as the *Dharmasastra* (written from about the seventh to the second centuries BCE) and the *Rg-Veda* (an orally transmitted text, composed in 900 BCE), Spivak emphasises that the practice of widow self-immolation is coded as an exceptional sacred practice, or pilgrimage, rather than an act of suicide (which is strictly forbidden in the terms of Hindu religious law):

> The two moments in the *Dharmasastra* that I am interested in are the discourse on sanctioned suicides and the nature of the rites for the dead. Framed in these two discourses, the self-immolation of widows seems an exception to the rule. The general scriptural doctrine is that suicide is reprehensible. Room is made, however, for certain forms of suicide which, as formulaic performance, lose the phenomenal identity of being suicide.
>
> (Spivak 1988: 299)

Traditionally, the act of taking one's own life is only permissable in the *Dharmasastra* if it is part of a sacred, religious pilgrimage; a privilege which is strictly reserved for men. As Spivak goes on to assert, however, '[r]oom is made' for the practice of widow sacrifice as an exceptional sacred practice, where the widow physically repeats her husband's death in a sacred place. Yet this exception to the strict rules of *sati* engenders a patriarchal structure of domination. As Spivak argues, 'the *proper* place for the woman to annul the proper name of suicide through the destruction of her proper self' is 'on a dead spouse's pyre' (Spivak 1988: 300).

Spivak reads this elaborate ritual as the legal displacement of the woman's subjectivity because such women are abdicated of legal responsibility for their own lives in the terms of Hindu religious codes. The woman's 'choice' to die is re-coded as an abdication of her free will. This legally displaced female subject is then re-defined as part of her husband's property in a sacred place, which is symbolised by the burning bed of wood or funeral pyre.

What is more, the event of *sati* symbolises an exemplary moment of woman's free will and moral conduct within Hindu culture: 'By the inexorable ideological production of the sexed subject, such a death can be understood as an *exceptional* signifier of her own desire, exceeding the general rule for a widow's conduct' (Spivak 1988: 300). As Spivak emphasises, the practice of widow self-immolation is not prescribed or enforced by Hindu religious codes, but is an 'exceptional signifier' of the woman's conduct as a good wife.

In the terms of British colonial legislation in India, this sense of widow sacrifice as an exceptional signifier of woman's conduct is lost in translation. For many British colonial administrators, the practice of *sati* epitomised the abhorrent and inhuman characteristics of Hindu society. By representing *sati* as a barbaric practice, the British were thus able to justify imperialism as a civilising mission, in which white British colonial administrators believed that they were rescuing Indian women from the reprehensible practices of a traditional Hindu patriarchal society. Indeed, the practice of *sati* was outlawed by the British colonial government in 1829.

In her discussion of *sati*, Spivak argues that the British colonial representation of widow self-immolation overlooks the voice and agency of Hindu women. For Spivak, this colonial representation is exemplified in *Suttee* (1927), a text written about widow self-immolation by the British colonial administrator Edward Thompson (1886–1946). Spivak argues that Thompson exacerbates the ideological constriction of those women by 'absolutely identifying, *within discursive practice*, good-wifehood with self-immolation on the husband's pyre' (Spivak 1988: 305). Such a claim repeats the silencing of the Hindu woman's voice, which is already displaced on to her dead husband's funeral pyre in the traditional Hindu religious codes described above. Rather than defending the woman's agency, however, the British colonial administration used the body of the widow as an ideological battle-ground for colonial power. In doing so the British were able to justify colonialism, or the systematic exploitation and appropriation of territory, as a civilising mission. In both the Hindu and British discussions of widow sacrifice, the voice and political agency of the woman is thoroughly repressed from official historical discourse and political representation.

Spivak's discussion of *sati* or widow sacrifice operates as an important counterpoint to western theories of political representation. As Spivak suggests, the complex construction of the legally displaced female subject within Hindu religious codes and the British constitution of the widow as a passive victim of patriarchal violence each ignore the social and political agency of the subaltern woman. It is in this context that Spivak argues that 'there is no space from which the sexed subaltern can speak' (Spivak 1988: 307).

Spivak further concludes that 'the subaltern cannot speak' (Spivak 1988: 308) because the voice and agency of subaltern women are so embedded in Hindu patriarchal codes of moral conduct and the British colonial representation of subaltern women as victims of a barbaric Hindu culture that they are impossible to recover.

SATI AND ANTI-COLONIAL INSURGENCY

Spivak supplements the longer analysis of *sati* in the colonial archives and the archives of Hindu antiquity with the discussion of Bhubaneswari Bhaduri, touched upon in Chapter 2. This young woman 'hanged herself in her father's modest apartment in North Calcutta in 1926' and Spivak goes on to contend that 'Nearly a decade later it was discovered that she was a member of one of the many groups involved in the armed struggle for Indian independence' (Spivak 1988: 307). Bhubaneswari had attempted to cover up her involvement with the resistance movement through an elaborate suicide ritual that *resembled* the ancient practice of Hindu widow sacrifice.

Technically, Bhubaneswari's suicide did not conform to the codes of widow self-immolation because Bhubaneswari was not a widow, and the suicide did not take place in the sacred site of a dead husband's funeral pyre. There is of course no way of proving with any certainty what Bhubaneswari Bhaduri's intentions were. Nevertheless, Spivak reads Bhubaneswari's story as an attempt to rewrite 'the social text of *sati*-suicide in an interventionist way' (Spivak 1988: 307). Spivak compares Bhubaneswari's attempt to rewrite the text of *sati* to the

HEGEMONY

The concept of hegemony was originally developed by the Italian Marxist philosopher and political leader Antonio Gramsci (1891–1937). After the failure of a workers' revolution in Italy, Gramsci questioned the classic Marxist view that a proletarian revolution was the *inevitable* consequence of the economic division of labour between the worker and the capitalist, and that ideology would disappear once capitalism was overthrown. Instead, Gramsci emphasised that dominant ideological institutions such as political parties, the church, education, the media and bureaucracy also play an important role – equal to that of the capital-labour contract – in maintaining relations of ruling. Against the classic Marxist notion of ideology as false consciousness, Gramsci thus proposed the more complex and flexible term *hegemony* to emphasise how people's everyday lives and identities are defined in and through dominant social structures that are relatively autonomous of economic relations. In the case of the 'hegemonic account of the fighting mother', the image of the woman as hero in the rhetoric of anti-colonial struggles can be seen to encourage women to freely participate in nationalist struggles for independence. The account of the fighting mother is hegemonic because it directly addresses the everyday lives of women as heroic mothers, in order to persuade them to participate in the anti-colonial resistance struggle.

The crucial difference between classic Marxist accounts of ideology and Gramsci's definition of hegemony is that classic Marxist accounts of ideology as 'false consciousness' suggest an element of manipulation, deception, even coercion; whereas hegemony depends on the consent and agreement of the individual.

'hegemonic account of the fighting mother' during national independence struggles in India (Spivak 1988: 308).

For Spivak, there is no question that Bhubaneswari was a politically committed and courageous member of the national independence struggle in India. Yet, as a 'model of interventionist practice' Spivak argues that Bhubaneswari's attempt to rewrite the text of *sati*-suicide is a 'tragic failure' (Spivak 1988: 307) because the 'subaltern as female cannot be heard or read' in the male-centred terms of the national independence struggle (Spivak 1988: 308). Spivak uses the metaphor of a 'palimpsest' to describe how Bhubaneswari's participation in the anti-colonial resistance struggle is erased by the supplementary narratives that try to re-tell her story. For Bhubaneswari's exceptional act of women's resistance during the independence struggle in the 1920s is disguised as an act of *sati*-suicide, and then later re-coded as a case of illicit love and a source of private shame for subsequent generations of her own family.

Spivak's statement 'the subaltern cannot speak' (Spivak 1988: 308) has generated much controversy about the limitations of contemporary theoretical paradigms, as well as political structures of representation. Indeed, critics such as Benita Parry (1987) have argued that Spivak's use of poststructuralist methodologies to describe the historical and political oppression of disempowered women has further contributed to their silencing. Writes Parry, 'Spivak in her own writings severely restricts (eliminates?) the space in which the colonized can be written back into history, even when "interventionist possibilities" are exploited through the deconstructive strategies devised by the post-colonial intellectual' (Parry 1987: 39).

Similarly, Bart Moore-Gilbert (1997) has argued in a commentary on Spivak's work that there are clear historical examples where the resistance of subaltern women in the colonial world is recorded in dominant colonial discourse: 'From Nanny, the guerrilla leader of the Maroon uprisings of 1773, through the bazaar prostitutes' role in the 1857 Indian "Mutiny" and the Nigerian market women protesters of 1929 to the "bandit queen" Phoolan Devi today, the resistance of the subaltern woman has always been acknowledged in dominant historiography' (Moore-Gilbert 1997: 107).

For Spivak, however, the crucial point is that these examples of subaltern resistance are always already filtered through dominant systems of political representation. As Spivak states in an interview, '"the subaltern cannot speak" means that even when the subaltern makes an effort to the death to speak, she is not able to be heard' (Spivak 1996: 292). This is not to suggest that particular disempowered groups cannot speak, but that their speech acts are not heard or recognised within dominant political systems of representation.

Spivak's conclusion that the subaltern cannot speak is often taken out of context to mean that subaltern women have no political agency because they cannot be represented. Such a reading is actually contrary to the very situated theoretical framework that Spivak establishes in 'Can the Subaltern Speak?'. Spivak would certainly not want to deny the social agency and lived existence of disempowered subaltern women. The crucial point, however, is that these disempowered women receive their political and discursive identities within historically determinate systems of political and economic representation.

CAN THE SUBALTERN VOTE?

Spivak's argument has been developed further in an essay by Leerom Medovoi, Shankar Raman and Benjamin Johnson, entitled 'Can the Subaltern Vote' (1990), which was published in the *Socialist Review*. Focusing on the Nicaraguan elections in 1990, the authors contest the common-sense notion that 'the immediacy of the speaker–listener relationship in everyday speech' can be applied to 'political speaking' (Medovoi *et al.* 1990: 133). Noting how, in the Nicaraguan elections, political representation was mediated by 'the workings of economics and power in the subordination of third-world countries' (Medovoi *et al.* 1990: 134), the authors argue that 'the electoral process actually reproduced the subalternity of the people at the very moment that it seemed to let them speak' (Medovoi *et al.* 1990: 134). They continue:

> Rather than hearing a complex statement regarding the political, economic, and military subordination of Nicaragua to US capital and geopolitics, the US press – and in some unfortunate respects even the US solidarity movement – heard what they took to be the simple voice of Nicaraguan sovereignty. Where Nicaraguans spoke out of an arduous double-bind of neocolonialism, North Americans often listened with touching faith in the timeless transparency of the electoral process.
>
> (Medovoi *et al.* 1990: 134)

By focusing on the limitations of the Nicaraguan elections from the perspective of the subaltern, Medovoi, Raman and Johnson help to clarify Spivak's argument about the limitations of political speech or representation in 'Can the Subaltern Speak?'. Indeed, Spivak has praised this essay as 'a fruitful way of extending my reading of subaltern speech into a collective arena' (Spivak 1999: 309).

Spivak does not offer any perfect political solutions or theoretical formulas for emancipating subaltern women, but rather exposes the limited and potentially harmful effects of speaking for such disem-powered groups. As the feminist ethnographer Kamala Visweswaran observes:

> Gayatri Spivak has asked the question 'Can the Subaltern Speak?' and answered with an unequivocal no. Speech has, of course, been seen as the priv-ileged catalyst of agency; lack of speech as the absence of agency. How then might we destabilize the equation of speech with agency by staging one woman's subject refusal as a refusal to speak?

> (Visweswaran 1994: 69)

Following the logic of Spivak's argument, Visweswaran challenges 'the equation of speech with agency' and suggests that the silence of the subaltern could be interpreted as a refusal to speak in the dominant terms of political representation.

More recently, in one of the most detailed and rigorous commen-taries published to date on 'Can the Subaltern Speak?', Sandhya Shetty and Elizabeth Jane Bellamy (2000) have located Spivak's historical inves-tigation of *sati* in relation to Jacques Derrida's subsequent work on the archive in *Archive Fever* (1995). In their view, Derrida's concept of the archive is 'crucial' for 'a more sympathetic understanding of Spivak's now notorious "silencing" of subaltern women' (Shetty and Bellamy 2000: 25). What is more, they argue that 'Can the Subaltern Speak?' transforms the private family secret of the circumstances of Bhubaneswari's suicide into the public archive of postcolonial studies (47).

Spivak's deconstruction of elite representations of the subaltern may not be satisfactory as a political goal in itself, but it does at least mark 'the danger of appropriating the other by assimilation' (Spivak 1988: 308). By foregrounding the historical and political determinants that shape representation, Spivak gradually moves from a negative emphasis on the impossibility of representation towards a more situated articula-tion of particular histories of subaltern insurgency and agency in the postcolonial world.

SUMMARY

- Spivak's theory of the subaltern is part of a longer history of left-wing anti-colonial thought that was concerned to challenge the class/caste system in India.
- Spivak's critique of the Subaltern Studies collective in 'Deconstructing Historiography', and her investigations of subaltern women's histories in 'The Rani of Sirmur' and 'Can the Subaltern Speak?', have radically challenged the terms and categories of political identity and struggle in contemporary thought.
- By rethinking the Marxist concepts of class struggle and class-consciousness through the critical lenses of deconstruction and feminism, Spivak has produced a more flexible and nuanced account of political struggle, which takes the experiences and histories of 'Third World' women into account.
- By foregrounding the aesthetic and political dimensions of representation, Spivak is able to mark the difference between her own role as postcolonial intellectual and the concrete, material lives of the subaltern. In doing so, Spivak has produced a better reading strategy that responds to the voices and unwritten histories of subaltern women, without speaking for them.

'THIRD WORLD' WOMEN AND WESTERN FEMINIST THOUGHT

Spivak's rearticulation of subaltern women's histories in 'Can the Subaltern Speak?', 'The Rani of Sirmur', and her commentaries on the writing of Mahasweta Devi have also radically transformed the terms and focus of western feminist thought. Indeed, one of the most important contributions that Spivak has made to contemporary feminist thought is her consistent demand that feminism seriously consider the material histories and lives of 'Third World' women in its account of women's struggles against oppression.

Spivak's contribution to feminist thought also includes essays on contemporary French feminist theory, nineteenth-century English women's writing, Marxist feminism and feminist critiques of political economy. Spivak's earliest essays on feminism were published during the 1980s, a time when the ideas of French feminist thinkers such as Julia Kristeva, Luce Irigaray and Hélène Cixous were first becoming available to the English-speaking world. In essays such as 'French Feminism in an International Frame' (1981) and 'Feminism and Critical Theory' (1986) Spivak offers original and engaging commentaries on these thinkers. Yet Spivak also raises important and challenging objections to the theoretical writing of French feminism.

In particular, Spivak challenges the universal claims of feminism to speak for all women. Together with the postcolonial feminist thinkers Chandra Talpade Mohanty, Rajeswari Sunder Rajan, Nawal El Saadawi and Kumari Jayawardena, Spivak has generated an important rethinking of feminist thought. Such a rethinking has challenged the assumption that all women are the same, and emphasised the importance of respecting differences in race, class, religion, citizenship and culture between women. This is not to suggest that Spivak is simply against feminism, or that Spivak is anti-feminist, however. On the contrary, Spivak's persistent critique of western feminist thought aims to strengthen the arguments and urgent political claims of feminist thought.

This chapter will begin by assessing the limitations and blind spots of western feminist theory. Focusing initially on Spivak's critique of French feminist theory, the chapter will then move to examine how Spivak has challenged the political claims of early Anglo-American feminist literary criticism from the critical perspective of 'Third World' women. Following on from this, the final section of the chapter considers Spivak's argument that women are the new source of cheap labour and super-exploitation by multinational corporations, based in the 'Third World'. By focusing on the plight of these women, Spivak has helped to redefine the critical terms and future goals of feminist politics.

Before considering exactly how Spivak's work has contributed to western feminist thought, it is important first of all to situate her work in relation to key debates in early feminist thought.

FEMINISM AND THE QUESTION OF DIFFERENCE

During the latter half of the twentieth century, early feminist social and political struggles had certainly advanced the democratic rights and freedoms of women in Europe and North America, but they had done so in the western philosophical tradition of liberal humanism. Humanism basically refers to the idea that all human beings are the same; that they share the same values; and should, in theory, have the same basic human rights. For European feminist thinkers such as Simone de Beauvoir (1908–86), however, liberal humanist thought had traditionally defined women as 'Other', or inferior to the universal humanist subject or 'Man'. The political task of early, so-called 'first- and second-generation' feminism thus focused on goals such as the women's franchise, equal pay, reproductive rights, and equality in the work place.

The tradition of universal humanist thought had further defined the difference between men and women as a natural fact, grounded in a

ESSENTIALISM

In philosophy, the term essentialism is commonly understood as a belief in the real, true essence of things, the invariable and fixed properties which define the 'whatness' of a given entity (Fuss 1989: i). More specifically, in Anglo-American feminist theory, anti-racist theory and gay/lesbian theory during the 1980s and early 1990s, the word essentialism came to have increasingly negative connotations because it defined categories like gender, race or sexuality in terms of fixed human essences, based on prior biological explanations. Such a theory of human identity is problematic because it runs the risk of ignoring particular cultural differences in race, class, sexuality, religion, ethnicity or identity. For this reason, critical thought in the 1980s and early 1990s generally shifted to an anti-essentialist position, which rejected all stable categories of identity. Hence for the anti-racist thinker Henry Louis Gates, race was redefined as a pernicious metaphor rather than a scientific truth claim; and for feminist theorist Judith Butler, sexuality and gender were rethought as social and linguistic constructs rather than stable biological foundations. Instead of fixed human essences and identities, anti-essentialist thought takes up more flexible positionings or positionalities in social, political and critical thought.

biological foundation that is prior to social and cultural influence. Simone de Beauvoir had discredited this view with the assertion that 'one is not born a woman, one becomes a woman'. For de Beauvoir, the category of gender identity was not determined by one's biological sex; rather gender is a social construct, which can be resisted through social and political struggle.

For recent 'anti-essentialist' feminist thinkers, Simone de Beauvoir's model of sex/gender does not go far enough. By leaving the biological category of sex unexamined, Beauvoir had failed to question the very scientific explanation (women's biological difference from men) that was used to justify women's oppression and discrimination. As Judith Butler argues in *Gender Trouble* (1990), the predominant understanding of sex as a biological category, which is *prior* to social and cultural influence, ignores how sex can *only* be made intelligible through the dominant discourses of medicine and the church, as well as the family and educational institutions. What Butler means by discourse in this context is not merely language, but the power of language in the hands of dominant social institutions to construct and determine human identity. For example, at the moment of childbirth, the midwife's assertion that 'it's a girl' immediately names and defines a child according to the rules and norms of a patriarchal society.

Like Butler, French feminist intellectuals such as Luce Irigaray (1939–) and Julia Kristeva (1941–) generally agree with de Beauvoir that the category of feminine identity is a social construct. However, this does not mean that gender identity can simply be resisted or avoided at will. Indeed, the discourse of gender identity is reinforced and regulated by powerful patriarchal institutions such as the Family, the State, Education, the Law and the Media.

For Spivak, the work of Luce Irigaray and Julia Kristeva has been very influential in redefining the terms of *western* feminist thought. In 'Feminism and Critical Theory', for example, Spivak argues that:

> My own definition of a woman is very simple: it rests on the word 'man' as used in texts that provide the foundation for the corner of the literary criticism establishment that I inhabit. You might say that this is a reactionary position. Should I not carve out an independent definition for myself as a woman?
>
> (Spivak 1987: 77)

Spivak's 'definition' recalls Luce Irigaray's argument in *This Sex Which is Not One* that 'For the elaboration of a theory of woman, men I think suffice' (Irigaray 1985: 123). Like Irigaray, Spivak suggests that 'independent' definitions of woman always risk falling prey to the very binary oppositions that perpetuate women's subordination in culture and society.

Against this binary system of thinking, Spivak proposes a critical strategy, which mimes the negative representation of minority groups such as women, the subaltern or the working class. Spivak refers to this critical strategy as strategic essentialism.

Spivak's contribution to contemporary feminist thought has certainly been informed by French feminist thinkers such as Luce Irigaray and Hélène Cixous. Yet Spivak has shifted the focus of the essentialist debate from a concern with sexual difference between men and women to a focus on cultural differences between women in the 'Third World' and women in the 'First World'.

In 'French Feminism in an International Frame' (1981), for instance,

STRATEGIC ESSENTIALISM

The idea of strategic essentialism accepts that essentialist categories of human identity should be criticised, but emphasises that one cannot avoid using such categories at times in order to make sense of the social and political world. In the place of an uncritical theory of essentialism, Spivak's early contributions to feminist and postcolonial theory (during the 1980s) proposed a 'strategic use of essentialism in a scrupulously visible political interest' (Spivak 1987: 205). For minority groups, in particular, the use of essentialism as a short-term strategy to affirm a political identity can be effective, as long as this identity does not then get fixed as an essential category by a dominant group. For example, the affirmation of queerness as a positive term of identification during Gay Pride marches can be an effective political strategy for resisting homophobia in public, urban space. Similarly, in 'New Ethnicities' (1988) Stuart Hall argues that the affirmation of ethnicity as a positive term of identification for different 'Black British' minority groups can be an effective strategy for redefining 'Englishness' and English culture from the standpoint of different minority groups. And in 'Under Western Eyes' Chandra Talpade Mohanty describes how 'Iranian middle-class women veiled themselves during the 1979 revolution [in Iran] to indicate solidarity with their working-class sisters' (Mohanty 1988: 78). This latter, context-specific strategy clearly challenges the common assumption that the veil is *always* a sign of women's oppression by repressive patriarchal Islamic laws. Yet as Spivak points out in an interview with Ellen Rooney about the question of strategic essentialism, 'a strategy suits a situation; a strategy is not a theory' (Spivak 1993: 4). Strategic essentialism is thus most effective as a context-specific strategy, but it cannot provide a long-term political solution to end oppression and exploitation.

Spivak identifies a tendency in some French feminist thought to describe the experiences of 'Third World women' in the terms of western female subject constitution. Such an approach clearly ignores some very important differences in culture, history, language and social class. Spivak develops this argument further in her reading of the short story 'Breast Giver' by Mahasweta Devi. In Spivak's argument, the experiences of Devi's subaltern female protagonist, Jashoda, challenge the assumption prevalent in western feminism that childbirth is unwaged domestic labour. In 'Breast Giver', Jashoda is employed as a professional mother in an upper-class Brahmin household to support her crippled husband, Kangali. As Spivak emphasises, Jashoda's reproductive body and breast milk are valuable resources which nourish the upper-class Haldar household, and are a source of income for Jashoda's crippled husband. Yet the continued exploitation of Jashoda's reproductive, maternal body finally causes her to suffer a painful death from untreated breast cancer. For this reason, Spivak argues that the fictional character Jashoda 'calls into question that aspect of Western Marxist feminism which, from the point of view of work, trivializes the theory of value and, from the point of view of mothering as work, ignores the mother as subject' (Spivak 1987: 258). Jashoda's experiences as a professional mother and wet nurse thus challenge the universal claims of western feminism to speak for all women.

UNLEARNING AND THE CRITIQUE OF WESTERN FEMINISM

The lives and struggles of 'Third World' women such as Jashoda may also seem far removed from the practice of reading literary texts or feminist theory in a university classroom. Yet for Spivak, this privileged distance from the lives of oppressed women in the 'Third World' does not mean that one should simply forget about the disempowered. Rather, Spivak emphasises how any act of reading (especially in the western university classroom) can have social and political consequences. In 'Practical Politics of the Open End', for example, Spivak argues that 'the manipulation of Third World labor sustain[s] the continued resources of the U.S. academy' (Spivak 1990: 97).

This materialist approach to reading is developed more explicitly in a conversation between Gayatri Spivak, Deepika Bahri and Mary Vasudeva about the limits of feminist reading practices with regard to the exploitation of women workers in homeworking economies. As Spivak states:

> The feminist anthology [...] overlooks completely this incredibly important issue of the most important example of gendering in neo-colonialism: women in homeworking – the women in export processing zones and export-based foreign investment factories, subcontracting areas.

> (Spivak 1996a: 72)

Rather than ignoring the political oppression of disempowered groups, Spivak has persistently challenged the sanctioned ignorance of western academic paradigms towards 'Third World' women through what she terms, a project of 'un-learning our privilege as our loss' (Spivak 1990: 9). This project involves recognising how dominant representations of the world in literature, history or the media encourage people to forget about the lives and experiences of disempowered groups.

The concept of unlearning in Spivak's work has also had a significant impact on feminist theory and criticism. In 'Under Western Eyes: Feminist Scholarship and Colonial Discourses' (1988) Chandra Talpade Mohanty has criticised a tendency in western feminist scholarship to 'colonize the material and historical heterogeneities of the lives of women in the Third World' (Mohanty 1988: 66). What is more, Mohanty argues that 'assumptions of privilege and ethnocentric universality on the one hand, and inadequate self-consciousness about the effect of western scholarship on the "Third World" in the context of a world system dominated by the west on the other, characterise a sizeable extent of western feminist work on women in the 'Third World' (Mohanty 1998: 66). In Mohanty's view, these 'assumptions of privilege and ethnocentric universality' can have a damaging effect on different women living in the 'Third World'.

An example of this problem is also seen in Mohsen Makhmalbaf's *Kandahar* (2001), a film which explores the position of women living in Afghanistan under the Taliban regime. Throughout the film, Makhmalbaf repeatedly emphasises how the wearing of a burka is an unequivocal sign of women's subjugation. The problem with such a cinematic representation is that it can reinforce a tragic stereotype of the 'Third World' woman as a passive victim, where *all* women who are seen to wear burkas or veils by western viewers will be regarded *a priori* as an oppressed group. As Mohanty emphasises, however, there are particular circumstances and contexts when women have deliberately chosen to wear the veil. As discussed above (see p. 75), during the Iranian revolution in 1979, middle-class women actively chose to wear the veil as a sign of solidarity with their working-class sisters. Similarly, during the Algerian War of Independence, Algerian women used the *haik* to conceal weapons and supplies in the struggle against the French colonial administration in Algeria. Such cases are addressed further in Frantz Fanon's book *A Dying Colonialism* (1970) and Gillo

Pontecorvo's film *The Battle of Algiers* (1966), and exemplify how women have actively participated in different anti-colonial resistance movements, and are not simply oppressed.

FRENCH FEMINISM IN AN INTERNATIONAL FRAME: SPIVAK ON KRISTEVA

Like Chandra Talpade Mohanty, Spivak has questioned the universal claims of some western feminists to speak for all women, regardless of cultural differences. In 'French Feminism in an International Frame' Spivak traces a narcissistic tendency in the French feminist thought of Julia Kristeva (1941–) to represent the histories and lives of Chinese women in the terms of western female subject constitution. Spivak prefaces this reading of Kristeva with a discussion of the limitations of western academic feminism from her own standpoint as an upper-class, educated Indian woman, who emigrated to the USA in the early 1960s. Spivak writes:

> The 'choice' of English Honors by an upper-class young woman in the Calcutta of the fifties was itself highly overdetermined. Becoming a professor of English in the US fitted in with the 'brain drain'. In due course, a commitment to feminism was the best of a collection of accessible scenarios.

> (Spivak 1987: 136)

As an educated woman, who graduated with a first-class English honours degree from the University of Calcutta, before going on to teach English literature in the USA during the 1970s and 1980s, Spivak's decision to commit to feminism can be seen to challenge the conservativism of English literary studies, both in the USA and India. Yet, Spivak's self-critical emphasis is also an attempt to make sense of the historical and social conditions which led to her emigration to the USA. Recalling a childhood memory of her grandfather's estate on the Bihar–Bengal border in the 1950s, Spivak describes overhearing a conversation between two 'washerwomen' about the ownership of the land by the East India Company. Because the material conditions of these women's lives had remained the same since the days of the East India Company, it had gone unnoticed that the land ownership had passed from the East India Company to the British Raj and then to the independent republic in India. At the time, Spivak had concluded that the women's description of the land was historically inaccurate, and that the independent republic in India now governed the land. Through a careful process of unlearning, however, the mature Spivak realises that this initial 'precocious' judgement of the women's situated knowledge of the land reflected Spivak's own class-based assumptions about the women.

Such a personal anecdote is not merely autobiographical, but situates Spivak's criticism of western feminism in relation to the historical experiences and everyday lives of disempowered women in the 'Third World'. The washerwomen's feeling that they have not been emancipated by decolonisation in India also serves to highlight the limitations of western feminism towards 'Third World' women. As Spivak asserts, '[t]he academic feminist must learn to learn from them' rather than simply correcting the historical experiences of disempowered women with 'our superior theory and enlightened compassion' (Spivak 1987: 135). Spivak thus cautions against the universal claims of western feminism, and emphasises instead how the specific material conditions, histories and struggles of 'Third World' women are often overlooked by western feminism. For Spivak, this problem is most strikingly exemplified in Julia Kristeva's book *About Chinese Women* (1977).

Spivak's critique of Julia Kristeva focuses initially on Kristeva's self-conscious description of a scene in Huxian, a village that is forty kilometres away from Xi'an, the first capital of China after it was unified in the second century BC (Kristeva 1977: 11). In this early section of the book, Kristeva describes an encounter between herself and a group of Chinese peasants in the village-square:

> An enormous crowd is sitting in the sun: they wait for us wordlessly, perfectly still. Calm eyes, not even curious, but slightly amused or anxious: in any case, piercing, and certain of belonging to a community with which we will never have anything to do.
>
> (Kristeva 1977: 11)

From this initial description of a face-to-face encounter with a village community in China, it might appear that Kristeva is concerned to engage with and learn from the historical and cultural experiences of the villagers. But as Spivak emphasises, Kristeva seems more concerned with how her own identity as a western woman is questioned in the face of the silent women in Huxian.

Such a focus on the crisis that encounters with different cultures bring to the western self is highlighted in Kristeva's subsequent question, 'Who is speaking, then, before the stare of the peasants at Huxian?' (Kristeva 1977: 15). For Spivak, Kristeva's questions exemplify a tendency in the work of some western poststructuralist intellectuals to invoke *other* cultures as a way of challenging the authority of *western* knowledge and subjectivity. As Spivak states:

> In spite of their occasional interest in touching the *other* of the West, of metaphysics, of capitalism, their repeated question is obsessively self-centred: if we are not what official history and philosophy say we are, who then are we (not), how are we (not)?
>
> (Spivak 1987: 137)

In the section entitled 'Who is Speaking?' Kristeva is anxious to distance her own project from earlier anthropological discourses which represent non-western cultures as primitive or backward. Such distancing takes place in part through a reversal of the lens that places non-western cultures in the western anthropologist's field of vision. Rather than focusing on the villagers as the *object* of anthropological inquiry, Kristeva initially recalls how the villagers perceive her as an outsider, or a foreigner.

Yet despite Kristeva's apparent commitment to touch 'the other of the West', Spivak argues that Kristeva's project remains 'obsessively self-centred' (Spivak 1987: 137). Indeed, Kristeva abandons her commitment to engage in a dialogue with the women at Huxian when she realises that any attempt to define the gaze of the peasants is futile (Kristeva 1977: 13), and does nothing to surmount the 'abyss of time and space' (Kristeva 1977: 11) that she perceives to separate the party of French intellectuals from the Huxian villagers.

Kristeva also identifies how her subjectivity as an educated, middle-class French-educated woman is 'moulded [. . .] by universal humanism, proletarian brotherhood, and (why not?) false colonial civility' (Kristeva 1977: 13). Such class and cultural determinants may appear to stifle the possibility of a cross-cultural dialogue with the Huxian villagers. Yet, by turning to the historical location of women in ancient Chinese society, Kristeva implies that an understanding of women's role in Chinese history will offer some access to the lives of the women peasants in Huxian.

Kristeva is attracted to the ancient matriarchal origins of China because they seem to provide an alternative feminist utopia that contrasts with the patriarchal monotheism of western thought. As Spivak contends, however, Kristeva's emphasis on Chinese women and *ancient* matrilinear social structures extrapolates the category of woman from other important social and cultural factors in *contemporary* China. By doing so, Kristeva shifts the focus away from the historically specific experiences and practices of women in China to discussions about western women.

For Spivak, Kristeva's self-centred discussion of Chinese women is further exemplified by the use of sweeping generalisations about women's historical position in China. For instance, Kristeva traces a significant break 'in the rules of kinship' in China which took place around 1000 BC (Kristeva 1977: 46). This break ostensibly marked a gradual transition from a matrilinear social structure, in which economic, territorial and social relations were regulated by the strongest woman in the community (Kristeva 1977: 48), to a patriarchal and feudal system. As Kristeva puts it: 'The Order of the Fathers replaces the Order of the Mothers, and the importance of the maternal uncle may be seen as a transitional step towards the patrilinear – and later patriarchal – institution of Confucianism' (Kristeva 1977: 58–9). By returning to this moment in ancient Chinese history, Kristeva emphasises how the transition from a matrilinear social system to a patriarchal, feudal economy was never completed, and that earlier elements of this ancient matrilinear structure have persisted throughout the history of China.

For Spivak, what is problematic about this re-reading of Chinese history is the way that ancient matrilineal kinship structures in China are lifted to support Kristeva's more general theory of the 'feminine'. Kristeva invokes the ancient Chinese matriarch to counteract the repression of women's bodies in the European psychoanalytic writing of Sigmund Freud (1856–1939) and Jacques Lacan (1901–81). As I will now briefly suggest, the real political concern in Kristeva's *About Chinese Women* is not the lived, material realities of peasant women in China, but the theoretical repression of women's bodily existence in European culture.

As Spivak argues in 'French Feminism in an International Frame' Kristeva is not primarily concerned with the historical position that women occupy within Chinese culture and society *per se*. Spivak contends that Kristeva's utopian view of the ancient Chinese matriarch effectively ignores the contemporary cultural practices of women in China: 'the "classical" East is studied with primitivistic reverence, even as the "contemporary" East is treated with realpolitikal contempt' (Spivak 1987: 138).

Citing the example of the Fall from the Garden of Eden in *Genesis*, Kristeva asserts how, in the Judaeo-Christian west, 'monotheistic unity is sustained by a radical separation of the sexes' (Kristeva 1977: 19). For Kristeva, this early example of sexual differentiation in western civilisation forms the basis for subsequent models of women's oppression.

From this brief comparison, it might appear that Kristeva's focus on women in China offers a powerful, utopian counterpoint to western theories of femininity in western culture. As Spivak emphasises, however, Kristeva's *About Chinese Women* illustrates a tendency of some western feminist thought to define the very particular experiences of 'Third World' women in the general terms of western women's sexual rights and political sovereignty. Noting Kristeva's utopian prediction for the 'sexual freedom' of Chinese women, Spivak criticises this 'prediction about China' on the grounds that it is 'symptomatic of a colonialist benevolence' (Spivak 1987: 138).

Indeed, Spivak is sceptical of whether Kristeva's model can actually benefit the lives of Chinese women at all, when the critical focus remains centred on the 'investigator as subject' (Spivak 1987: 150). As Spivak argues, 'Institutional changes against sexism [in the USA] or in France may mean nothing, or indirectly, further harm for women in the Third World' (Spivak 1987: 150). To counter this imposition, Spivak proposes an additional focus to the questions Kristeva asks in Huxian Square.

Such a focus would ask the following questions: 'Not merely who am I? But who is the other woman? How am I naming her? How does she name me?' (Spivak 1987: 150). Without these crucial questions, Spivak insists that the '"colonized woman" as subject' in Kristeva's model will 'see "feminism" as having a vanguardist class fix, the liberties it fights for as luxuries, finally identifiable with "free sex" of one kind or another' (Spivak 1987: 150).

For Spivak, Kristeva's revolutionary characterisation of women's sexual desire is too straightforward, and ignores important cultural and class differences between women. Instead, Spivak tries to chart a more sophisticated map or 'geography of female sexuality'.

THE GEOGRAPHY OF FEMALE SEXUALITY

In 'French Feminism in an International Frame' Spivak questions whether the valorisation of women's non-reproductive sexual pleasure in French feminist thought is an effective political goal for 'Third World' women. Invoking the practice of clitoridectomy in certain parts of Sudan, Spivak questions the Eurocentric assumption that clitoridectomy is exclusively a ritual imposed on 'Third World' women 'in remote and primitive societies' (Spivak 1987: 151). Spivak emphasises instead that 'symbolic clitoridectomy', or the repression of female sexuality, 'has always been the "normal" accession to womanhood and the unacknowledged name of motherhood' (Spivak 1987: 151). By re-defining clitoridectomy as the symbolic repression of *all* female sexual pleasure, Spivak thus suggests that clitoridectomy is the general condition of women's social and economic oppression.

What is at stake in Spivak's discussion of clitoridectomy is how the 'effacement of the clitoris, of women's sexual pleasure [. . .] can be considered a metonymy of women's social and sexual status' (Grosz in Spivak 1990: 10). Put more simply, the dominance of patriarchal social relations depends on the definition of women's reproductive bodies as the legal objects, or private property, of men. Clitoridectomy thus refers to the symbolic effacement of women's non-reproductive sexual desire as a way of reproducing patriarchal dominance.

Against this effacement of women's non-reproductive sexual desire, Spivak proposes the following critical task:

> Investigation of the effacement of the clitoris – where clitoridectomy is a metonym for women's definition as 'legal object as subject of reproduction' – would persistently seek to de-normalize uterine social organization.
>
> (Spivak 1987: 152)

By investigating the 'effacement of the clitoris' Spivak tries to demonstrate how patriarchal social relations have objectified women's reproductive bodies. Yet in doing so, Spivak recognises that there is a danger that feminism will be perceived as an exclusively western movement, which does not recognise the plight of women in the 'Third World'. Against this perception, Spivak develops a more situated framework that focuses on the different ways that women's reproductive bodies are objectified on both sides of the global political economy.

In the 'First World', 'the uterine norm of womanhood' provides the support for 'the entire advanced capitalist economy' which 'hinges on home buying' and 'the sanctity of the nuclear family' (Spivak 1987: 153). In the 'less developed countries', Spivak argues that the 'repression of the clitoris as the signifier of the sexed subject [. . .] operates the specific oppression of women, as the lowest level of the cheap labor that the multi-national corporations employ by remote control in the extraction of [profit]' (Spivak 1987: 153).

One of Spivak's clearest accounts of the geography of female sexuality is seen in her reading of Devi's short story 'Breast Giver', which has already been mentioned several times. Against French feminist theorists who valorise women's non-reproductive sexual pleasure as a universal strategy for women's political resistance, Spivak argues that in 'Breast Giver' 'we see cancer rather than the clitoral orgasm as the excess of the woman's body' (Spivak 1993: 90). 'Breast Giver' dramatises the exploitation and gruesome death of Jashoda, a subaltern woman character in Devi's historical fiction, who is employed as a professional mother and a wet nurse in the upper-class household of the Haldar family in post-independence Bengal. Spivak carefully follows Devi's descriptions of Jashoda's cancerous body in the closing sequence of the story, especially the phrase, 'The sores on her breast kept mocking her with a hundred mouths, a hundred eyes' (Spivak 1987: 260). For Spivak, the Sanskrit root of the Bengali word for mockery (*byango*) is deformed (Spivak 1987: 260). In this reading, the materiality of Jashoda's cancerous maternal body is thus seen to mock and deform the bourgeois nationalist metaphor of Mother India. What is more, Jashoda's revolting and cancerous maternal body offers a powerful and situated counterpoint to the universal valorisation of the clitoral orgasm as a space for women's embodied resistance and political struggle by some French feminist theorists.

'THREE WOMEN'S TEXTS' AND A CRITIQUE OF FEMALE INDIVIDUALISM

Spivak's demand for a geography of female sexuality is developed further in 'Three Women's Texts and a Critique of Imperialism' (1985), an essay that was published in the US journal *Critical Inquiry*. This essay may seem to depart from Spivak's earlier critique of French feminist theory (published in 1982), and her commentaries on

DISCOURSE AND COLONIAL DISCOURSE STUDIES

The study of discourse was originally developed by the French philosopher Michel Foucault (1926–84). In Foucault's view, discourse is not simply a body of words and sentences, but the very structure in which the social world is constructed and controlled as an object of knowledge. What is more, Foucault argued that 'it is in discourse that power and knowledge are joined together' (Foucault 1978: 100). The study of discourse is thus inseparable from the study of institutional power, discipline and domination in western societies. In *Orientalism* (1978) Edward Said expands Foucault's analysis of regimes of discourse, power and knowledge in western societies by applying this model to what he calls orientalism, or **colonial discourse**. Like Foucault, Said emphasises how the will to know and understand the non-western world in colonial discourse is inseparable from the will to power over that world. For Said, western colonial power over the non-western, 'Oriental' world is maintained in and through the discourses of the arts, humanities and social sciences, as well as through more direct forms of domination such as political rule and military repression. As Robert Young asserts in a commentary on Said's use of the word discourse:

> Said's deployment of the concept of a 'discourse' for his analysis of Orientalism enabled him to demonstrate a consistent discursive register for particular perceptions, vocabularies and modes of representation common to a wide variety of texts extending across the humanities and social sciences – from travel accounts to history, from literature to racial theory, from economics to autobiography, from philosophy to linguistics. All these texts could be analysed as sharing a consistent colonial ideology in their language as well as their subject matter, a form of knowledge that was developed simultaneously with its deployment and utilization in a structure of power, namely colonial domination.
>
> (Young 2001: 388)

Colonial discourse analysis thus dissolves the neat distinction between cultural texts and institutional or political discourses, emphasising instead how all texts that represent the colonial world are implicated in a structure of colonial power and knowledge.

Mahasweta Devi, because it focuses on nineteenth-century British fiction. Yet, there are some important similarities between these essays, as I will discuss in a moment.

The 'three texts' to which the title refers include Charlotte Brontë's novel *Jane Eyre* (1848), Jean Rhys's novel *Wide Sargasso Sea* (1966) and Mary Shelley's novel *Frankenstein* (1818). I will say more about Spivak's reading of *Wide Sargasso Sea* in the closing chapter of this book. For the purpose of this chapter, however, I want to consider how Spivak's reading of *Jane Eyre* traces a hidden imperialist sub-text in Jane Eyre's narrative of bourgeois female individualism. By tracing this history, Spivak challenges Anglo-American feminist readings of *Jane Eyre*, which celebrate Jane's heroic narrative of self-determination to the exclusion of Bertha Mason's colonial genealogy. Spivak reads these three literary texts as part of a larger system of colonial discourse; a critical approach which is tacitly informed by the thought of Michel Foucault and Edward Said.

Like Said, Spivak approaches *Jane Eyre*, *Frankenstein* and *Wide Sargasso Sea* as examples of colonial discourse, and collapses the boundaries between fictional discourse and the discourse of institutional and political power. 'Three Women's Texts' initially considers the way in which British literary classics such as Charlotte Brontë's *Jane Eyre* (1848) have gained cult status in contemporary Anglo-American feminist literary criticism because the text privileges the individual narrative of its main female protagonist, Jane Eyre. Examples of such a reading of *Jane Eyre* include Sandra Gilbert and Susan Gubar's text *The Madwoman in the Attic* (1979) and Nancy Armstrong's *Desire and Domestic Fiction* (1987). By focusing on the narrative of Jane Eyre, Anglo-American feminist literary criticism repeats the narrative representation of Jane Eyre as a liberated western female individual.

As Spivak emphasises, however, this tendency to focus exclusively on Jane's first-person narrative overlooks the historical significance of Bertha Mason, the white Jamaican Creole woman, who is imported into the novel's gothic sub-plot as Jane's monstrous double (the 'mad' first wife of Rochester, the man Jane will later marry), and denied existence as a human individual. Alarmingly, this representation of Bertha Mason as an unknowable Other who is 'not yet human' (Spivak 1985: 247) recalls Kristeva's description of the unknowable stare of the peasants at Huxian square in *About Chinese Women*. Like the Chinese women Kristeva describes, Bertha Mason is denuded of any cultural or historical being, operating instead as an Oriental Other who reflects the stability of Jane's western female self. In Spivak's account, both of these texts reproduce the stereotypes of colonial discourse in the representation of western female individualism.

Another connection between 'French Feminism in an International Frame' and 'Three Women's Texts and a Critique of Imperialism' is the patriarchal definition of women's reproductive bodies. In 'French Feminism in an International Frame', 'clitoridectomy stands as a metonym for women's definition as "legal object as subject of reproduction"' (Spivak 1987: 152). In the nineteenth-century Victorian setting of *Jane Eyre*, the practice of 'childbearing' (Spivak 1985: 244) is framed within a domestic ideology that places women in a socially and economically disempowered position. This definition of the woman as an object of private property was legitimated in the terms of English common law, as well as Hindu Law (as we saw in Chapter 3). It is against this domestic ideology that Jane struggles to determine her reproductive body in the novel. Moreover, Jane's heroic narrative of self-determination in a patriarchal world has led many subsequent feminist critics in the twentieth century to invoke *Jane Eyre* as a proto-feminist literary text.

Such re-readings have been crucial for the development of western feminist literary criticism, but they only tell one side of the story. As Spivak emphasises, the individual rights and freedoms that are afforded to Jane Eyre in Brontë's novel are at the same time denied to Bertha Mason:

> As the female individualist, not quite/not male, articulates herself in shifting relationship to what is at stake, the 'native female' as such (*within* discourse, *as* a signifier) is excluded from any share in this emerging norm.
>
> (Spivak 1985: 245)

Spivak's reading of *Jane Eyre* locates the narrative of 'feminist individualism in the age of imperialism' (Spivak 1985: 244). In so doing, Spivak is able to account for the fundamental gender inequalities between Bertha and Jane. Whereas Jane's narrative of female individualism is coded in the domestic terms of marriage and childbearing, Bertha is defined by the 'axiomatics of imperialism' (Spivak 1985: 247). In other words, Bertha Mason is denied access to the category of female individual in the novel because of her Jamaican Creole lineage.

For Spivak, Bertha's predicament illustrates how nineteenth-century feminist individualism was not confined to women's struggles for reproductive rights within the 'closed circle of the nuclear family' (Spivak 1985: 248), but also contributed to a 'soul-making' enterprise in Britain's colonised territories (Spivak 1985: 244). What Spivak means by this phrase ('soul-making') is that the enlightened morality of the western female individual in the domestic sphere simultaneously defined the non-western woman as a 'not-yet-human Other' (Spivak 1985: 247). To situate this more precisely within the Victorian world of *Jane Eyre*, Jane stands as a paragon of feminine virtue, against whom Bertha Mason is defined as monstrous, or bestial, because of her mixed-race genealogy and wild, sexualised passion. This othering of the non-western woman has contributed to the larger justification of British imperialism as a social mission, or a soul-making enterprise, because it implicitly defines British cultural values as more enlightened and civilised than those of the colonial world.

It is not insignificant that the social mission of British imperialism concentrated on the gender coding of non-western women such as Bertha Mason. As Spivak points out, the formation of gendered identity in the nineteenth century is re-worked by colonial discourse, so that the white European female individual is defined as socially and culturally superior to the non-western woman. For Spivak, this social inequality between women is brought to the forefront in the relationship between Jane Eyre and Bertha Mason. If Jane struggles to define her individual autonomy within the narrow domestic sphere of Victorian Britain, Bertha Mason's identity is determined by the legal terms of her marriage to Rochester and subsequent domestic confinement in the attic of Thornfield Hall. For it is only when Bertha attempts to transgress the subject position of 'good wife' that she is cast as a monstrous inhuman figure. As Spivak points out, this understanding of Bertha's subjectivity is latent in *Jane Eyre*, but it is made manifest in Jean Rhys's rewriting of *Jane Eyre* from Bertha's point-of-view in *Wide Sargasso Sea*: 'In Rhys' retelling, it is the dissimulation that Bertha discerns in the word "legally" – not an innate bestiality – that prompts her violent reaction [to Rochester]' (Spivak 1985: 250).

This legal definition of Bertha's reproductive body as the private property of Rochester prefigures Spivak's later 1988 discussion of *sati* in 'Can the Subaltern Speak?' (discussed at length in Chapter 3). Indeed,

Spivak actually alludes to this essay at the end of 'Three Women's Texts and a Critique of Imperialism'.

To recap, in 'Can the Subaltern Speak?' Spivak argues that nineteenth-century British colonial administrators in certain parts of India redefined the Hindu practice of *sati* as widow self-immolation, rather than good wifely conduct. By presenting *sati* as a barbaric cultural practice, British colonial administrators were thus able to justify imperialism as a social mission.

The significance of *sati* in *Jane Eyre* becomes clear when one considers that the legal definition of women's reproductive bodies as private property is the *general condition* of female subject constitution in many patriarchal societies. Like Hindu Law, an ideology of good wifely conduct was also prevalent in British society, under the terms of English common law. For Spivak, this ideology is covered over in *Jane Eyre*, but it is foregrounded in *Wide Sargasso Sea*. By comparing the scene in *Jane Eyre* where Bertha violently attacks Richard Mason and the parallel scene in *Wide Sargasso Sea*, Spivak emphasises how in Rhys's retelling, Bertha Mason's violent reaction against Richard Mason is prompted by her brother's invocation of the legally binding marriage contract between Bertha and her husband Rochester, which defines Bertha as Rochester's private property. In *Wide Sargasso Sea*, the marriage of Bertha Mason to the British landowner, Rochester, illustrates how the violence of this ideology of 'good wifely conduct' was also manifest in the nineteenth-century Victorian world of *Jane Eyre* (Spivak 1985: 250).

Significantly, the legislative definition of Bertha Mason as the private property of her husband also recalls Spivak's earlier (1981) discussion of symbolic clitoridectomy in 'French Feminism in an International Frame' (discussed above). Just as the British colonial administration in India represented *sati* as a sign of the essential barbarism of Hindu culture in order to justify British colonial rule, so some western feminists have represented clitoridectomy as a barbaric ritual which is confined to primitive patriarchal societies in the 'Third World'. By tracing a historical relay between nineteenth-century bourgeois female individualism and twentieth-century western feminism, Spivak thus argues that the history of western feminism is complicit in the project of imperialist expansion.

SUMMARY

As Spivak argues in 'French Feminism in an International Frame' and 'Three Women's Texts and a Critique of Imperialism', the history of western feminism is implicated in the larger history of European colonialism. As a consequence, contemporary western feminism is in danger of repeating the colonial attitudes of nineteenth-century bourgeois female individualism towards 'Third World' women. This argument – that western feminism has been historically complicit in the project of imperialist expansion – is one of the most difficult and troubling aspects of Spivak's contribution to feminist thought. To counter this problem, Spivak repeatedly emphasises the following points:

- the important political and intellectual transformations that western feminism has achieved;
- the crucial need to challenge the universal humanist assumption, prevalent in some western feminist thought, that all women's lives and histories are the same;
- the importance of strategic essentialism for rethinking feminist thought from the perspective of different non-western women's lives and histories;
- the ongoing need to guard against colonial thinking in contemporary feminist scholarship and the importance of learning to learn from below;
- the importance of a *global* political awareness of the *local* economic, political, social and cultural conditions that structure women's oppression in different parts of the world.

5

MATERIALISM
AND VALUE

As I suggested in the previous chapter, Spivak's thought has generated a rethinking of western feminist thought from the perspective of women in the postcolonial world. One of the central ways that Spivak's work has enabled this shift in focus is by showing how disempowered women in the postcolonial world are the 'new focus of superexploitation' (Spivak 1987: 167).

To account for this contemporary form of women's economic oppression, Spivak reworks the traditional Marxist vocabulary of the division of labour between the worker and the capitalist, and situates women's economic exploitation in relation to the international division of labour between the 'Third World' and the 'First World'. By invoking this argument, Spivak demands that readers are familiar with debates in materialist thought, as well as feminist theory. More specifically, this aspect of Spivak's thought assumes a knowledge of the economic writings of the nineteenth-century German philosopher Karl Marx (1818–83).

This chapter begins by situating Spivak's engagement with Marx in relation to contemporary critiques of Marx. Then, the chapter considers how Spivak's sophisticated rethinking of Marx's writings on value, labour and capitalism has transformed the contemporary understanding of materialist thought. Finally, I will argue that Spivak's re-reading of Marx demonstrates the continuing importance of Marx's critique of

MARX AND IDEOLOGY

The crucial point that Karl Marx emphasises throughout his writings is that all areas of social life, including politics, religion, education, the media, arts and culture, are shaped and determined by economic relations. As Marx stated in 'Preface to A Critique of Political Economy' (1859), 'It is not the consciousness of men that determines their being, but on the contrary, their social being that determines their consciousness' (Marx 1977: 389). For Marx, the task of contemporary philosophy is to examine the real, material conditions of everyday life rather than higher, abstract ideals such as truth, beauty, spirit or consciousness. Indeed, Marx argued that these latter categories help to construct a dominant ideology, which obscures the real, material, economic conditions of human life under capitalism. For this reason, Marx defines ideology as 'false consciousness' or an imaginary representation of real social relations.

Subsequently, Marxist critics have emphasised that Marx's model of ideology is too reductive because it expresses all social relations in terms of economics. This problem is often referred to as economic determinism or reductionism. To counter this problem in Marx's thought, the twentieth-century French Marxist philosopher Louis Althusser (1918–90) argued that the superstructure, or the level of ideology, was relatively autonomous from the base, or the level of economics. In Althusser's account, the relative autonomy of the superstructure (culture, education and the media) from the economic base leaves room for people to question and challenge dominant, ideological representations of the social world. More recently, the 'post-Marxist' thinkers Ernesto Laclau and Chantal Mouffe have abandoned the base/superstructure model in Marx's definition of ideology. Against the economic determinism of Marxist thought about ideology, which privileges the monolithic white male working-class subject, Laclau and Mouffe have emphasised the importance of other social movements which cannot be accounted for in the narrow terms of economic relations. Such movements include, for example, feminism, anti-colonialism, anti-racism, and anti-globalisation. Like Laclau and Mouffe, Spivak has also emphasised the importance of negotiating and revising the terms of classic nineteenth-century Marxist discussions of ideology in the present, but has added that the economic cannot be rejected altogether in the contemporary context of global capitalism and the international division of labour.

capitalism to the political and economic legacy of colonialism and the international division of labour.

RETHINKING MARX

Since the collapse of the Soviet communist bloc in the late 1980s and early 1990s, the writing of Karl Marx has been widely perceived as irrelevant and outmoded by many political thinkers and economic theorists because Marx's ideas no longer seem to have any obvious or direct relationship to contemporary social and economic life in the western world. Yet, for other contemporary intellectuals, including Gayatri Spivak, Samir Amin, David Harvey, and Ernesto Laclau, the reasons for revisiting Marx's key ideas in the twenty-first century have never been more apparent. For the brutal labour conditions under which many women workers and child labourers are employed in the postcolonial world stand as painful examples of how Marx's critique of capitalism in nineteenth-century Europe is still relevant to the contemporary economic world.

One of the drawbacks to Karl Marx's thought was that he restricted his analysis of capitalism to Europe. Although Marx was certainly aware of European colonialism in the nineteenth century, he never really incorporated his writings on India and Africa into a developed analysis of imperialism. This omission has led many thinkers, including Edward Said, to criticise Marx's European-centred model of social change and political emancipation on the grounds that it ignores the plight of colonised subjects in non-western societies. Nevertheless, despite these problems, Marxism has provided a central intellectual and political framework for many postcolonial theorists and 'Third World' activists to negotiate and define particular forms of domination and resistance in the postcolonial world. As Robert Young contends:

> Anti- and postcolonial thought has always been engaged in a process of reformulating, translating and transforming Marxism for its own purposes, and this has operated as a critical dynamic tradition within Marxism itself. [. . .] If postcolonial theory is the cultural product of decolonization, it is also the historical product of Marxism in the anti-colonial arena. For many of the first generation of postcolonial theorists, Marxist theory was so much their starting point, so fundamental to what they were doing, so dominant in contemporary intellectual culture, that it was assumed as a base line prior to all further work.
>
> (Young 2001: 168)

The main reason why anti- and postcolonial thought is invested in this reformulation of Marxist thought is because of the historic failure of 'Third World' independence movements to achieve economic independence from the 'First World'. As Young further emphasises, the Bandung conference in 1955 was a foundational moment in the assertion of *political* independence for many 'Third World' nation states, but this did not lead to the economic independence of these countries from massive debt repayments to 'First World' banks. It is in the context of the 'Third World' debt and the contemporary international division of labour that Spivak's re-reading of Marx after Derrida should be understood.

Like Edward Said, Spivak is certainly aware of the problem of Eurocentrism in Marx's thought. In *A Critique of Postcolonial Reason*, for example, Spivak criticises Marx's writings on India for trying to insert non-Europe into a 'Eurocentric normative narrative' (Spivak 1999: 72). Yet at the same time, Spivak does not dispense with the categories and concepts of Marxist thought entirely. Instead, Spivak returns to some of the most nuanced discussions in Marx's later writing on value and political economy in order to demonstrate the continuing importance of Marx's thought to discussions of contemporary culture, politics and economics in a postcolonial context.

READING MARX AFTER DERRIDA

Before addressing Spivak's re-reading of Marx in more detail, it is important to remember that Spivak usually approaches Marx's writing through the lens of Jacques Derrida's deconstructive philosophy. One of Spivak's first published engagements with Marx took place in 1981 at a conference on deconstruction and politics in France. This paper, entitled 'Il faut s'y prendre en s'en prennant à elles' ('He Should Go About It by Blaming Them First' [my translation]), was subsequently developed by Spivak into an ongoing dialogue between the philosophical discourses of Marxism and deconstruction. These essays include: 'Speculations on Reading Marx: After Reading Derrida' (1987a), 'Scattered Speculations on the Question of Value' (published as an article in 1985; collected in Spivak 1987), 'Limits and Openings of Marx in Derrida' (1993) and 'Ghostwriting' (1995).

At times, Spivak's deconstructive approach to reading Marx may seem to shift the focus away from the political imperative to rethink

Marxist thought in a contemporary context towards a more rigorous philosophical reading of Marx. As Spivak acknowledges, 'to go via Derrida toward Marx can be called a "literary" or "rhetorical" reading of a "philosophical" text' (Spivak 1987a: 30). Yet such objections overlook how Marx was concerned to question the neat divisions between the practice of reading and the demand for political change. This split between theory and politics has been further questioned by Thomas Keenan in a related commentary on Marx's preface to *Capital Volume One*:

> *Capital* begins with a warning about failing to move from knowing directly on to doing, and about the temporal structure of the desired articulation. In reading, time will tell [. . .] but time to read is always also time to stop reading. Against the eagerness of a reading that wants to skip over the interpretation to get to the change, that wants to know how to relate general principles to immediate questions, Marx advises that articulation takes patience.
>
> (Keenan 1997: 102)

The very reason that Spivak employs a deconstructive critique of Marx's later economic philosophy is precisely to guard against the impatient and dogmatic interpretations of Marx's work, which have come to be associated with orthodox Marxist–Leninism and Soviet communism. The problem with such readings, as Keenan points out, is that they move too quickly from the act of interpretation to the demand for political change. Such readings are often based on partial and reductive readings of Marx's entire thought, which cite the urgency and political idealism of Marx's earlier writings to exemplify Marx's intellectual and political position. In texts like *The Communist Manifesto* (1848), for example, Marx certainly argued that a universal, revolutionary working-class subject would spring inevitably from the social contradictions that were manifest in nineteenth-century societies based on European industrial capitalism. However, in later works, such as the *Grundrisse* (1857) and *Capital* (1867), Marx was less optimistic about the immediate possibility of a socialist revolution, and modified his earlier utopian claims in favour of a more rigorous economic and philosophical analysis of nineteenth-century capitalism.

Marx's early model of revolutionary struggle outlined in *The Communist Manifesto* is clearly too narrow and inflexible to account for the diverse social movements of the twentieth century which have subsequently protested against the brute force and injustice of contemporary capitalism. In this context, Spivak's engagement with Marx after Derrida can be read as challenging Marx's early thought on philosophical and ethical grounds: on philosophical grounds because the early 'humanist' Marx suggested that the working-class struggle for economic equality and political emancipation in nineteenth-century Europe represented the political interests of all humanity, in all places, and at all times; on ethical grounds because the universal claims that were made in the name of the industrial working class in Europe excluded other disempowered groups, including women, the colonised, and the subaltern.

Spivak's re-reading of Marx focuses instead on Marx's later economic writings in *Capital* and the *Grundrisse*. There are two reasons why Spivak turns to the later Marx. First, Spivak sees a radical proto-deconstructive movement in Marx's later writing which challenges the critique of Marx's earlier utopian thought by deconstructive thinkers, such as Jacques Derrida. Spivak frequently emphasises that her reading of Marx after Derrida responds to a failure in Derrida's thinking to sufficiently address Marx's central argument about industrial capitalism in *Capital*. As Spivak writes in 'Limits and Openings of Marx in Derrida': 'Derrida seems not to know Marx's main argument. He confuses industrial with commercial capital, even usury; and surplus-value with interest produced by speculation' (Spivak 1993: 97). In this respect, Spivak's rethinking of Marx's later writing may seem to contribute to an ongoing theoretical debate about the politics of deconstruction, or the relationship between Marxism and deconstruction.

Yet, Spivak's debate with Derrida about Marx is not merely a question of philosophical rigour, and this leads to the second reason why Spivak turns to the later Marx. For Spivak's re-reading of Marx's later economic writing is also importantly grounded in the concrete gesture to the contemporary exploitation of women's (re)productive bodies in the 'Third World'. As Spivak writes in *A Critique of Postcolonial Reason*, 'Marx's prescience is fulfilled in postfordism and the explosion of global homeworking. The subaltern woman is now to a large extent the support of production' (Spivak 1999: 67). At times, Spivak's focus may seem to privilege the superexploitation of women's labour in the 'Third World' by transnational corporations as a 'true' proletarian position under contemporary global capitalism. Yet, this focus is not only an attempt to correct the male-centred, and European-centred focus of

Marxist thought. As I will now briefly suggest, Spivak's rethinking of Marxist thought is precisely a response to the changing gendered and geographical dynamics of contemporary capitalism itself.

FROM NINETEENTH-CENTURY EUROPEAN CAPITALISM TO THE CONTEMPORARY INTERNATIONAL DIVISION OF LABOUR

During the nineteenth century, industrial production tended to be concentrated in European cities. The conditions of labour for many working-class men in this context were very exploitative. However, the concentration of production in one place did allow these mostly male workers to gradually organise and protest against issues such as the length of the working day, safety in the workplace and low wages. It was precisely the economic conditions of working-class men in Europe that informed much of Marx's later economic writing. Even though Marx was certainly aware of European colonialism in India and Africa, and the unwaged labour of women in the domestic sphere, his descriptions of alienated labour and capitalist exploitation privileged the experiences of male workers under nineteenth-century European industrial capitalism.

For Spivak, by contrast, the conditions of contemporary economic exploitation are quite different. In the pursuit of even larger profits, contemporary multinational corporations tend to sub-contract production and manufacturing to places where workers are perceived to be the most vulnerable, non-unionised and therefore ripe for economic exploitation. In 'Feminism and Critical Theory' (1982), for example, Spivak describes how a group of women workers in a factory based in Seoul, South Korea, but owned by Control Data, a US based multinational, went on strike for a wage increase in 1982 (Spivak 1987: 89). The union leaders were subsequently dismissed and imprisoned; in retaliation, the women workers 'took hostage two visiting U.S. vice-presidents, demanding reinstatement of the union leaders' (Spivak 1987: 89). The dispute was ended when the 'Korean male workers at the factory beat up the female workers' (Spivak 1987: 89). For Spivak, this narrative is a powerful example of how global capitalism operates by employing working-class women in developing postcolonial countries. For not only do these women workers have no effective union representation, or protection against economic exploitation, but their gendered bodies are also disciplined in and through patriarchal social relations, including those of the family, religion, or the state. As Spivak states in 'Scattered Speculations on the Question of Value':

> It is a well-known fact that the worst victims of the recent exacerbation of the international division of labour are women. They are the true surplus army of labour in the current conjuncture. In their case, patriarchal social relations contribute to their production as the new focus of super-exploitation.
>
> (Spivak 1987: 167)

Because of the geographically dispersed conditions of contemporary capitalism it is very difficult for 'Third World' women workers to organise and represent themselves in the conventional political and philosophical terms that were available to working-class men in nineteenth-century Europe. What is more, Spivak's emphasis on how women's productive bodies are now a primary site of exploitation under contemporary transnational capitalism necessitates a re-thinking of the conventional male-centred, European definition of the working-class subject in Marxist theory.

RE-THINKING THE WORKING-CLASS BODY

Spivak (1992) makes this point more explicitly in an essay on the Indian writer Mahasweta Devi's short story 'Douloti the Bountiful' (1995). In this story, Devi offers a harrowing portrayal of a subaltern woman's exploitation in bonded labour and prostitution during the period of colonialism and subsequent national independence in India. In the final scene of this story, Douloti's 'tormented corpse' is depicted as being sprawled across a map of India, drawn by a schoolmaster in a rural village in India, just after independence from the British Empire. Despite the emancipatory promises of national independence, Devi emphasises how older forms of gender and class-based exploitation – such as bonded labour and prostitution – continue to be practised in postcolonial India.

Spivak goes further than this in the reading of Devi's story, arguing that Douloti's brutalised body not only highlights the limitations of national liberation in India, but also the contemporary international division of labour. Pointing to the common usage of the word 'doulot' in Bengal (meaning 'wealth'), Spivak emphasises that the proper name

'Douloti' has the connotation 'traffic in wealth' (Spivak 1992: 113). Reading the last sentence of Devi's short story in the original Bengali '*Bharat jhora hoye Douloti*' ('The traffic in wealth is all over India'), Spivak suggests that this sentence is a homophone of the phrase '*Jagat jhora hoye Douloti*' ('The traffic in wealth is all over the globe'). In the slippage between phonetically similar phrases, Spivak suggests a different interpretation of the story that is based on the notion that the subaltern woman's body is not only a site of exploitation in post-independence India (the postcolonial nation), but also in the contemporary global capitalist economy (the globe). As Spivak writes:

> Such a globalization of douloti, dissolving even the proper name, is not an overcoming of the gendered body. The persistent agendas of nationalisms and sexuality are encrypted there in the indifference of superexploitation, of the financialization of the globe.
>
> (Spivak 1992: 113)

I will discuss Spivak's translation work and commentary on Mahasweta Devi further in Chapter 6. But what concerns me in this chapter is how the embodied knowledge of the subaltern woman crucially informs Spivak's rethinking of Marx's economic and political philosophy.

SPIVAK, MARX AND THE LABOUR THEORY OF VALUE

Spivak opens her essay 'Scattered Speculations on the Question of Value' (1987) with a discussion of the philosophical concept of the subject in the German philosophy of G.W.F. Hegel and Karl Marx. Spivak writes:

> One of the determinations of the question of value is the predication of the subject. The modern 'idealist predication of the subject' is consciousness. Labour-power is a 'materialist' predication.
>
> (Spivak 1987: 154)

In this quoted passage, Spivak uses the grammatical word 'predication' to emphasise that the subject (in the materialist and the idealist predications, or constructions) is passive rather than active. Idealism or materialism constructs or predicates the subject as consciousness or labour power; she does not construct herself. This introductory discussion recalls Marx's earlier critique of Hegel in *The Economic and Philosophical Manuscripts* (1844) and his later formulation of a materialist notion of the subject in *The German Ideology* (1846) and the 'Preface to A Critique of Political Economy' (1859). In this latter text, Marx famously asserted that 'It is not the consciousness of men that determines their being, but on the contrary, their social being that determines their consciousness' (Marx 1977: 389).

In Marx's view, Hegel's model of dialectical thinking mystified the social and economic relations that were fundamental to an understanding of human identity. For Hegel, dialectical thought was a formal philosophical procedure that involved the reconciliation of opposing ideas. The goal of Hegel's dialectical method was to sublate or cancel out the human subject's non-relationship to the objective world in order to advance to a place of absolute self-knowledge.

Whereas Hegel argued that the alienation of the human subject could be resolved through abstract philosophical reflection (idealism), Marx emphasised that the alienation of the human subject was a historical product of the social division of labour between the ruling class and the working class (materialism). Turning Hegel's dialectical method on its head, Marx tried to show how the structural contradictions inherent in capitalism would eventually lead to the self-destruction of capitalism and the subsequent emancipation of all human subjects from the condition of alienation.

Since the collapse of the former Soviet Union and the communist bloc in the late twentieth century, and the subsequent integration of many socialist states into a global capitalist economy, many commentators have concluded that Marx's analysis of capitalism was wrong. Yet as Spivak points out in an interview (cited below), this conclusion ignores the rhetorical nuances of Marx's later writing on value and its continuing relevance to the contemporary international division of labour between the 'First World' and the 'Third World'.

In an interview with Sarah Harasym published in *The Post-Colonial Critic*, Spivak emphasises that if one attends carefully to Marx's reading of value in *Capital Volume One*, then 'there is a possibility of suggesting to the worker that the worker produces capital, that the *worker* produces capital because the worker, the container of labour power, is the source of value' (Spivak 1990: 96). From this initial statement, Spivak proceeds

IDEOLOGY AND VALUE

Marx's definition of ideology as 'false consciousness', or the imagined representation of real social relations, was originally proposed in *The German Ideology*. Marx went on to expand and develop this definition of ideology, along with his argument that the alienation of the individual from the product of her own labour is a defining characteristic of everyday life in capitalist societies. In *Capital Volume One*, Marx outlined his Labour Theory of Value, which basically described how profit (or surplus value) is made by paying workers less money in exchange for the greater amount of productive work which they actually perform during the working day. Marx starts by arguing that the products of human labour (or commodities) can be valued in two ways: as something to be used (a use value) or something to be exchanged (an exchange value). In the exchange of two objects with different uses (let's say a table and a chair), however, there has to be a general equivalent (such as money) which is capable of measuring the value of each object independently of its use. Marx refers to this general equivalent as exchange value. In Marx's formulation, value is calculated by subtracting the use value of an object from its exchange value. At a first glance, this definition may appear to be perfectly rational and fair. Yet, as Marx emphasises, the subtraction of use value from the exchange value of a commodity simultaneously strips the commodity of the human labour and natural resources that went into its production. As a consequence, the value of a commodity is nothing except a false representation of alienated human labour.

to argue that 'by the same token it is possible to suggest to the so-called "Third World" that it *produces* the wealth and the possibility of the cultural self-representation of the "First World"' (Spivak 1990: 96). By relating Marx's theory of value in the nineteenth century to the contemporary international division of labour between the 'First World' and the 'Third World', Spivak insists on the continuing importance of Marx's labour theory of value to contemporary readings of culture and politics.

Spivak develops this argument more fully in 'Scattered Speculations on the Question of Value' (1985), an argument that I will now briefly elaborate. Spivak initially turns to Marx's discussion of value in Chapter 1 of *Capital Volume One*, a key section of Marx's thought, in which Marx begins to develop the theory of the commodity. Spivak notes how 'Marx left the slippery concept of "use value" untheorized' (Spivak 1993: 97). For Marx, the concept of use value refers to the valuation of an object according to its particular material qualities.

Yet capitalism is not interested in the particular quality or usefulness of a singular object, but only in the exchange of objects for profit. As Marx noted, the value of a commodity is not defined according to an inherent property or use value of the object, but rather by abstracting its use value from its exchange value. A concrete example of this process of abstraction can be seen in the contemporary production and consumption of Nike athletic shoes. The price, or exchange value, of Nike athletic shoes is defined by their form of appearance as magical objects on television commercials. As a consequence, the exchange value of the shoes is disembodied, or abstracted, from the sweated labour conditions which many women workers in Indonesia and China are forced to endure in Nike's athletic shoe manufacturing lines. In Marx's terms, the process of abstraction strips use value of any particular meaning or significance in the exchange of commodities. Just so, the representation of Nike athletic shoes on television commercials encourages consumers to forget about the sweated human labour of many 'Third World' women which enables the production of such commodities.

Indeed, what is crucial for Marx is that the process of abstracting exchange value from use not only effaces the particular material quality of an individual commodity; but that it also effaces the human labour power necessary to produce those commodities. In short, the actual human labour necessary to produce a commodity is stripped from the content of a commodity when it is being exchanged. As Marx writes:

> With the disappearance of the useful character of labour, the useful character of the kinds of labour embodied in them also disappears; this in turn entails the disappearance of the different concrete forms of labour. They can no longer be distinguished, but are all together reduced to the same kind of labour, human labour in the abstract.

> (Marx 1976: 128)

Marx defines the residue of human labour that is left over from this process of abstraction as 'phantom-like' because it defies rational understanding: it cannot be named or identified as a positive concept.

Spivak foregrounds this ghostly, ambivalent definition of use value in the first pages of Marx's *Capital Volume One* as a starting point from which to challenge contemporary readings of Marx. The problem with many interpretations of Marx is that they tend to define value either in terms of a pure use value which is outside of exchange – 'the place of use-value [. . .] offers the most secure anchor of social 'value' (Spivak 1987: 161) – or else exclusively in terms of the exchange relationship, so that all traces of human labour are erased from the commodity. As Spivak points out, both explanations tend to ignore the ambivalent status of use value in Marx's definition of value. As a consequence of this misreading, the ghostly body of abstract human labour is forgotten about, and the transformation of exchange value into money and capital circulation is represented as an inevitable and totalising process.

For Spivak, this reductive reading of value as either pure use or pure exchange overlooks the ghostly presence of human labour in Marx's discussion of use value. By attending to this ambivalent status of use value in the Marxian text, Spivak questions the logical foundations which present capitalism as natural and inevitable. By doing so, Spivak suggests that the system of capitalist circulation can be interrupted and perhaps even subverted.

In this respect, Spivak may seem to follow the terms of Marx's argument. Yet this comparison overlooks important differences between the philosophical and political positions of Marx and Spivak. For Marx, the use value of human labour is defined as a *point of contradiction* between the worker and the capitalist. In Marx's historical narrative of progress, this point of contradiction between the worker and the capitalist would be finally resolved at a determinate point in the future when socialism completely overthrows capitalism.

Spivak criticises the logic of contradiction and historical inevitability that informs Marx's labour theory of value because it is based on a stable opposition between capitalism and socialism. Instead, Spivak emphasises how the ghostly presence of human labour operates as 'the possibility of an indeterminacy' (Spivak 1987: 160). Spivak's critique of Marx's reductive binary opposition between capitalism and socialism is informed by Jacques Derrida's deconstruction of binary oppositions in western philosophy. In *Of Grammatology* (1976), Derrida contends that there is a tendency in the history of western philosophy since Plato to treat speech as a pure, authentic and true expression of human

consciousness, and writing as a corrupt, inauthentic and false representation of speech. In a way that is parallel to Derrida's deconstruction
of the speech/writing dichotomy, Spivak rejects the romantic anti-
capitalist idea that use value is simply a pure, unalienated expression of
the worker's labour power and that exchange value is a corrupt, alien-
ating representation of capitalist exploitation. Although the analogy
between writing and value is not perfectly symmetrical, the crucial
point is that use value is inextricably part of exchange value. In other
words, the sphere of exchange and capital circulation is haunted by the
spectre of labour and the productive body of the worker.

By emphasising this ambivalent, ghostly status of use value (as neither
one thing nor another), Spivak thus destabilises those critiques of Marx
that rewrite 'value as exchange value and exchange value alone' (Chow
1993a: 3). But how does this emphasis on the ambivalence of use value
in Marx's *Capital* relate to the urgent political and economic questions
that Spivak raises about the gendered international division of labour?
To understand how Spivak's careful philosophical reading of Marx
relates to these urgent political considerations, it is helpful to situate
Spivak's reading of Marx in relation to other recent engagements with
Marx's thought.

THE CRITIQUE OF ECONOMIC DETERMINISM

One of the limitations of Marx's economic writings was that Marx
had privileged the division of labour between the male worker and
the capitalist in European societies as a structuring principle in social
relationships. The French philosopher Louis Althusser described this
relationship between economics and social relations as economic
determinism because Marx had defined all social relations as a reflection of the capitalist division of labour. As a consequence of this
economic determinism, other forms of social oppression are left out
of Marx's theoretical model: including those based on gender, race
and sexuality. Because Marx generally ignored these social groups,
many twentieth-century commentators, including Louis Althusser,
Etienne Balibar, Judith Butler, Michel Foucault, Fredric Jameson,
Stuart Hall, Donna Haraway and Ernesto Laclau, shifted the focus of
Marxist thought away from economics to questions about the way
that human identity is constituted in and through ideology and
discourse.

This focus on the constitution of human identity in discourse and ideology has transformed the terrain upon which radical political struggles are negotiated, both in theory and in practice. Yet as Spivak emphasises, this rethinking of Marxist thought during the 1960s and 1970s in western cultural studies cannot be separated from the major economic and social transformations that were taking place in the postcolonial world during that time. In the context of capitalism's global expansion in the postcolonial world, Spivak thus invokes Walter Benjamin's 'famous saying, "there has never been a document of *culture* which is not at one and the same time a document of barbarism"' (Spivak 1987: 167). Walter Benjamin's statement is often taken as a critique of the idea that culture transcends the material conditions of its production. For Benjamin, writing as a Jewish intellectual in Nazi Germany, the very idea of culture as a separate sphere that is autonomous from social and political relations is dangerous because it obscures the truth of human suffering and oppression under real material conditions of barbarism. Spivak modifies the meaning of Benjamin's statement to emphasise that the tendency to focus on culture and identity in western cultural studies to the exclusion of economics overlooks contemporary forms of barbarism, such as western foreign policy in the Middle East or South Asia and 'free' trade agreements with Latin America, Indonesia and South Korea. As Spivak argues: '"a culturalism" that disavows the economic in its global operations cannot get a grip on the concomitant production of barbarism' (Spivak 1987: 168). More importantly, Spivak re-asserts the importance of the economic in critical and cultural theory by emphasising how the exploitation of women workers in the 'Third World' provides the wealth and resources for intellectual culture in the 'First World'.

This is a very different argument from the classic Marxist position that privileges the male, working-class subject as the main historical protagonist for economic and political change. Indeed, Spivak is careful to distinguish her own position from the economic determinism of Marx by insisting on a deconstructive approach that places the economic 'under erasure' (Spivak 1987: 168). By crossing out the word economic in this context, but retaining its visibility, Spivak emphasises that the word 'economic' no longer has the same negative connotations of determinism; instead the economic focus of Marxism is crucial for a critical understanding of contemporary globalisation and the international division of labour.

Spivak's re-articulation of Marx's later economic writings thus demonstrates the critical and political importance of Marx's labour theory of value to the contemporary global economic system. As Spivak suggests, one of the limitations of postmodern readings of Marx, in the work of Jean Baudrillard or Jean Joseph Goux for instance, is that their analysis of value and the logic of capitalism is produced from the standpoint of developed, industrialised nation states in the 'First World'. Even when European postmodern thinkers (such as Jean Baudrillard or Georges Bataille) do focus on non-western economies, they tend to invoke these economies as primitive conceptual objects for western theorising rather than examining how postcolonial/'Third World' nation states have been integrated into the global capitalist economic system. The problem with such postmodern theories of value is that they clearly overlook how workers in the developing economies of postcolonial nation states such as Mexico, India or Indonesia produce the wealth and resources for powerful nation states in the contemporary western world. Indeed, Spivak argues that 'any critique of the labour theory of value, pointing at the unfeasability of the theory under post-industrialism, or as a calculus of economic indicators, ignores the dark presence of the Third World' (Spivak 1987: 167).

More specifically, Spivak asserts that it is working-class women in the 'Third World' who are 'the worst victims [. . .] of the inter-national division of labour' (Spivak 1987: 167). To support this argument, Spivak invokes a concrete example comparing the profits of a large multinational corporation and the earnings of a woman in Sri Lanka:

> [W]hereas Lehman Brothers, thanks to computers, earned about $2 million for [. . .] fifteen minutes of work, the entire economic text would not be what it is if it could not write itself as a palimpsest upon another text where a woman in Sri Lanka has to work 2,287 minutes to buy a t-shirt. The 'post-modern' and 'pre-modern' are inscribed together.
>
> (Spivak 1987: 171)

Spivak's discussion of the gendered and geographical dynamics of contemporary global capitalism may not seem to be directly related to discussions of contemporary culture. Yet, this is precisely the point. By focusing on these economic questions Spivak reminds readers of how the so-called '"Third World" [. . .] *produces* the wealth and the

possibility of the cultural self-representation of the "First World"'
(1990: 96). In foregrounding the importance of Third World women's
productive bodies in the geographical dynamics of contemporary global
capitalism, Spivak thus emphasises how this economic text is inscribed
and embedded in the production and reception of all contemporary
culture.

DECONSTRUCTING *CAPITAL*

To recap, the logic of contemporary global capitalism attempts to efface
the use value of the subaltern woman's labour power. Yet, as Spivak
emphasises, it is precisely the use value of the subaltern woman's
productive body which provides a cheap, dispensable resource for the
accumulation of wealth in the First World. Indeed, it is precisely
through a careful reading of Marx's labour theory of value that Spivak
demonstrates the indispensable relevance of Marx's nineteenth-century
Labour Theory of Value to the labour conditions of women workers
in the Third World, and thus to the economic and social relations of
global capitalism.

In 'Openings and Limits of Marx in Derrida', Spivak develops this
argument further, by making the important distinction between the
capital relation and capitalism. Recalling Marx's argument in *Capital
Volume Three* that capital accumulation is indispensable to socialism,
Spivak writes that:

> [T]here is no philosophical injustice in the [capital relation]. Capital is only the
> supplement of the *natural* and *rational* teleology of the body, of its irreducible
> capacity for superadequation, which it uses as its use value.
>
> (Spivak 1993: 107)

Simply put, capitalism uses the human body's natural surplus energy so
that the capitalist gets more labour than he actually pays for. But in this
transaction between worker and capitalist, the capitalist does not simply
coerce the human subject to work harder for less. For unlike the conditions of slavery or feudalism, in the capital relation the worker is a free
agent who consents to sell her surplus labour power to the capitalist.
Thus, in western philosophical terms, there is no social injustice in the
capital relation because capital is only a rational extension of the human
body's ability to produce more than it needs to survive.

Of course, this is not to say that Spivak is arguing that capitalism is a just or fair economic system. What Spivak does make clear, however, is that Marxism cannot account for the social injustice of capitalism in the terms of its own philosophical system. As Rey Chow observes in a commentary on Spivak's reading of Marx:

> The interest of [Spivak's] reading of Marx is that there is something philosophy cannot account for, no matter how 'consistent' it is – or precisely because it is so 'consistent'. This something is the asymmetry between capital and labour, the accounts of which have to be settled outside the bounds of philosophy's sense of justice.

(Chow 1998: 36)

It is precisely because philosophy cannot account for this 'asymmetry between capital and labour' that Spivak approaches the Marxian text through the critical lens of deconstruction. For deconstruction is precisely concerned with impossible concepts such as justice or ethics which cannot be calculated in advance according to a set of pre-defined rules or criteria. Like justice and ethics, value is also an incalculable concept; it is neither pure use nor pure exchange and disrupts the stable opposition between socialism and capitalism. Spivak thus traces those incalculable moments in Marx's discussion of value which are the condition of possibility for a future social justice and political transformation. In 'Supplementing Marxism' (1995a), for example, Spivak argues that:

> [S]ocialism is not in opposition to the form of the capitalist mode of production. It is rather a constant pushing away – a differing and a deferral – of the *capital*-ist harnessing of the social productivity of capital.

(Spivak 1995: 119)

By emphasising how socialism cannot manage without the capital relation, Spivak deconstructs the binary opposition between capitalism and socialism, which has traditionally grounded classic Marxist theories of emancipation. As Spivak makes clear in 'Ghostwriting' (1995), this attempt to rethink the opposition between labour and capital in a post-colonial context is not an original idea in the history of 'Third World' political thought. Rather, this deconstruction of capitalism/socialism continues the longer debate about the need to define a 'Third World' alternative to capitalism and communism, which was started at the

Bandung Conference in 1955 and the Movement of Non-Aligned Countries in 1961. Robert Young has suggested that the Bandung conference was a foundational moment in the assertion of political independence by many 'Third World' nation states (Young 2001: 191). Yet, as Spivak emphasises, this political independence has not led to the economic independence of many 'Third World' countries from huge national debt repayments to 'First World' banks and the gendered international division of labour. What is more, Spivak argues that the ideals of a New International since Bandung (later enshrined in the 1974 UN Declaration for the Establishment of a New Economic Order) have proved to be absolutely useless in opposing the current legalised economic exploitation of lower-class women in the 'Third World' by the world trade agreements and organisations such as the General Agreement on Tariffs and Trade (GATT) and the World Trade Organisation (WTO). Instead, Spivak points to the sub-national struggles of local resistance movements: to 'the specter of Marxism that has been at work, molelike, although not always identified with Left parties in the impotent State' (Spivak 1995: 69–70). It is in the context of these contemporary political and economic debates that Spivak's re-reading of Marx after Derrida should be understood.

SUMMARY

- Reading Marx after Derrida, Spivak redefines the political task of Marxist critique as an ethical call to read Marx patiently and carefully.
- At times Spivak reads Marx more as a philosopher than as an economist, focusing on his systems and critique of capitalism. Yet, Spivak's rethinking of Marx through deconstruction always also emphasises the need to retain a sense of the economic in contemporary cultural analysis.
- Spivak traces the ghostly presence of human labour contained in Marx's verbal presentation of the capital relation. What is more, Spivak is asking readers to remember that it is the labour of 'Third World' women in particular which is exploited in the contemporary global capitalist economy.
- In doing so, Spivak demonstrates the direct relevance of Marx's Labour Theory of Value to the contemporary International Division of Labour.

For many readers the political imperative to read Marx carefully may seem difficult, if not impossible. Yet, this political project is only impossible in the narrow, philosophical terms of value determination, where the exploitation of the woman worker in the 'Third World', like that of Marx's (male) industrial worker, cannot be represented as such. This does not mean that these people do not exist. Indeed, Spivak's persistent attempt to deconstruct the capitalist system of value determinations is not simply a corrective theoretical reading of Marx, but an urgent call to articulate the cultural, political and economic conditions which silence the 'Third World' woman in the hope that those oppressive conditions will eventually change.

6

COLONIALISM, POSTCOLONIALISM AND THE LITERARY TEXT

Literature, or the teaching of literature, has been instrumental in the construction and dissemination of colonialism as a ruling idea. In *Masks of Conquest: Literary Study and British Rule in India*, Gauri Viswanathan argues that 'the discipline of English came into its own in the age of colonialism' and that 'no serious account of its growth and development can afford to ignore the imperial mission of educating and civilizing colonial subjects in the literature and thought of England' (Viswanathan 1987: 2).

Gayatri Chakravorty Spivak's literary criticism has greatly informed and influenced the practice of reading literary texts in relation to the history of colonialism. In essays such as 'Imperialism and Sexual Difference' (1986), 'Three Women's Texts and a Critique of Imperialism' (1985), and 'The Rani of Sirmur' (1985a), Spivak examines how the civilising mission of imperialism was written and disseminated in and through several classic texts from the English literary tradition, including Daniel Defoe's *Robinson Crusoe* (1719), Charlotte Brontë's *Jane Eyre* (1847) and Mary Shelley's *Frankenstein* (1818), as well as a historical narrative from the colonial archives of the East India Company. Like Edward Said and Homi Bhabha, Spivak repeatedly emphasises that the production and reception of nineteenth-century English literature was bound up with the history of imperialism. In 'Three Women's Texts and a Critique of Imperialism', Spivak argues that literature provided a cultural representation of England as civilised and progressive: an idea which served to justify the economic and political project of imperialism.

This chapter begins by examining Spivak's colonial discourse analysis in her readings of the German philosopher Immanuel Kant (1724–1804) and Charlotte Brontë's *Jane Eyre*. This latter section expands on the earlier discussion of *Jane Eyre* in Chapter 4 by focusing on Spivak's reading of the fictional character St John Rivers in relation to the civilising mission of imperialism. Discussion then moves to Spivak's readings of postcolonial texts which challenge the authority of colonial discourse. Finally, the chapter carefully examines Spivak's textual commentaries on and English translations of the fiction of Mahasweta Devi.

SPIVAK AND COLONIAL DISCOURSE ANALYSIS

The focus of Spivak's criticism is not restricted to nineteenth-century English literary culture and the historical context of imperialism. In marked contrast to the colonial discourse analysis of critics such as Edward Said, who tend to focus on dominant literary texts from the European literary tradition, Spivak has also demonstrated the rhetorical and political agency of postcolonial literary texts to question and challenge the authority of colonial master narratives. It is perhaps for this reason that Spivak's name is often associated with postcolonial criticism. The postcolonial texts that Spivak has engaged with include writing by the Algerian feminist writer Assia Djebar, the British writer Hanif Kureishi, the India-born British writer Salman Rushdie and the Bengali-language fiction writer, Mahasweta Devi. By so doing, Spivak could be seen to complicate the totalising model of colonial discourse that some critics have attributed to Edward Said's *Orientalism* (1978).

Basically, the problem with Said's early model of colonial discourse was that it seemed to offer a very persuasive theory of how the west knows, controls and dominates the non-west through an all-encompassing system of representation, but it did not offer an effective account of political resistance, or the 'real', material histories of anti-colonial resistance that were masked by this dominant system of western representation. Admittedly, Said has subsequently revised his model of colonial discourse in the light of subsequent criticism by Dennis Porter and Aijaz Ahmad (among many others). Yet as Bart Moore-Gilbert emphasises, there is still a tendency in Said's thought towards a uniform vision of Western Orientalism (Moore-Gilbert 1997: 75). By contrast, Moore-Gilbert suggests that Spivak 'offers a more complex vision of the effects of western domination' (76), and that she tends to focus more 'on various manifestations of counter-discourse' (75).

Without understating the repressive and violent effects that colonialism has had on non-western cultures, Spivak frequently insists on the need to situate the particular experiences of colonialism in a precise historical and cultural context. What is more, Spivak's engagement with postcolonial literary texts that rewrite the master narratives of European culture has provided an important critical vocabulary and theoretical framework for reading and valuing texts that articulate the multivalent cultural histories and practices of different non-western cultures.

Before assessing Spivak's contribution to postcolonial literary criticism, however, it is important to consider Spivak's critique of colonial discourse in more detail.

THE RHETORIC OF COLONIALISM

The success of British colonial rule in India during the nineteenth century was not only dependent on the threat of military force, but also on the sophisticated use of rhetoric to convince the educated, Indian middle-class elite that British culture was more civilised and therefore a more superior form of government. By winning the support of the Indian middle-class political elites in the mid nineteenth century, the British were thus able to rule by consent, rather than through direct military force. If colonial rule was managed through bureaucratic, economic and political institutions, it was culture – especially literature and philosophy – that provided the rhetorical basis for western colonial expansion.

Indeed, for Spivak the civilising mission of European colonialism is itself founded on the use of culture as a form of rhetoric. Drawing on the deconstructive criticism of Paul de Man, Spivak argues that 'the basis of a truth claim is no more than a trope' (Spivak 1986: 225). In classical rhetoric, a trope is a figure of speech in which one thing is used to talk about another. For de Man, philosophical truth claims are marked and constituted by the effacement of tropes. Spivak develops de Man's argument to show how the suppression of rhetoric in the production of truth claims can have damaging consequences in a broader social and political field. More specifically, Spivak argues that deconstruction's concern with the constitution of truth in philosophical discourse can be usefully applied to the 'axiomatics of imperialism' (Spivak 1999: 19). Focusing on key texts from the European philosophical enlightenment tradition, as well as from European literature, Spivak carefully follows the rhetoric of those texts to highlight instances where ideas, concepts, or metaphors are deployed as the truth within the broader historical and geographical context of imperial expansion.

An exemplary case of this reading strategy is Spivak's engagement with the eighteenth-century German philosopher Immanuel Kant, published in *A Critique of Postcolonial Reason* (1999). In this text, Spivak announces in advance that her reading of Kant's three *Critiques* will be a 'misreading' (Spivak 1999: 9). Such a strategy of deliberate misreading draws on Paul de Man's argument that all texts are aware that they are figurative and are therefore open to misreading. In Spivak's account, de Man's practice of reading involves a double movement. The first step of this movement is the 'discovery that something that claims to be true is a mere trope', and the second step 'disclose[s] how the corrective impulse within the tropological analysis is obliged to act out a lie in attempting to establish it as the corrected version of truth' (Spivak 1999: 19). For Spivak, the lie that the German philosopher Immanuel Kant performs to define the rational human subject in *The Critique of Judgement* involves the erasure of a racialised figure, whom Kant refers to as the raw man.

Rather than adhering rigidly to the narrow philosophical questions that Kant addresses, Spivak traces the imperialist determinants that underwrite Kant's theory of the human subject in *The Critique of Judgement*. As Spivak puts it: 'The subject as such in Kant is geopolitically differentiated [. . .] Kant's text cannot quite say this and indeed cannot develop this argument' (Spivak 1999: 27). Spivak's assertion that 'Kant's text cannot quite say this' is important because it guides the reader through Spivak's own deconstructive reading practice: a practice that is informed by Paul de Man's argument that the rhetorical character of *all* language (whether philosophical or literary) opens up the possibility of misunderstanding (de Man 1983: 136).

KANT AND THE CIVILISING MISSION OF IMPERIALISM

In order to better understand the deconstructive operations of Spivak's theoretical approach to colonial discourse, it is helpful first of all to follow Spivak's engagement with the textual operations of Kant's text. Spivak begins her reading of Kant by summarising the key philosophical arguments of Kant's three *Critiques*:

> Kant's *Critique of Pure Reason* charts the operation of the reason that cognises nature theoretically. *The Critique of Practical Reason* charts the operation of the rational will. The operations of the aesthetic judgement [in *The Critique of Judgement*] allow the play of concepts of nature with concepts of freedom.
>
> (Spivak 1999: 10)

As Spivak suggests, there is an irreconcilable contradiction between *The Critique of Pure Reason* and *The Critique of Practical Reason*, where the moral subject is bound to the determining structures of reason: 'The human being is moral only insofar as he cannot cognise himself' (Spivak 1999: 22). Kant attempted to resolve this contradiction through the aesthetic category of the sublime. In Kant's philosophical schema, the sublime refers to the feeling of pain that occurs when the individual human imagination encounters itself in relationship to the non-representable magnitude of the natural world, yet is able to conquer this feeling of pain through recourse to the rational faculties of the human mind. In other words, the sublime provides an aesthetic structure for rational and cultivated human subjects to conquer their fear of unrepresentable concepts such as the infinite and death.

One of the fundamental rational faculties that Kant invokes in his discussion of the sublime is that of culture. In *The Critique of Judgement*, Kant argues that it is primarily cultivated and educated men who can make judgements about taste and sublimity. For Spivak, this moment in Kant's argument is particularly revealing because it raises questions about those groups and societies who *do not* have access to the culture that Kant is describing. For if the moral subject needed culture to define *his* cognitive limitations in the face of the infinite structure of the sublime, what happens to those subjects who do not have access to Kant's understanding of morality or culture?

As Spivak argues, Kant's reading of the sublime presented itself differently to those people who were not represented as moral subjects within Kant's European philosophical system: 'Without development of moral ideas, that which we, prepared by culture, call sublime presents itself to man in the raw [*dem rohen Menschen*] merely as terrible' (cited in Spivak 1999: 12–13). Spivak picks up on the German adjective '*roh*' in Kant's text, noting that while it is normally translated as 'un-educated', the term 'uneducated' in Kant's work specifically refers to 'the child and the poor'; the 'naturally uneducable' refers to women; and '*dem rohen Menschen*, man in the raw', connotes 'the savage and the primitive' (Spivak 1999: 13).

Spivak further proceeds to argue that Kant's theory of the universal subject, or 'Man', does not refer to all humanity, but only refers to the educated, bourgeois, masculine subject of the European enlightenment. Citing a passage from Kant's discussion of the sublime in *The Critique of Judgement*, Spivak notes how Kant excluded the 'Australian aborigine or the man from Tierra del Fuego' from the category of human subjectivity in his analytic of the sublime. By so doing, Spivak links Kant's philosophical discussion of the 'raw man' in his account of the sublime to the 'axiomatics of imperialism': 'we find here the axiomatics of imperialism as a natural argument to indicate the limits of the cognition of (cultural) man' (Spivak 1999: 26).

For Spivak, the 'axiomatics of imperialism' refers to the self-evident truth, which western imperialism claims as its self-justifying basis. Spivak thus suggests that the narrow European-centred definition of the moral subject in the world of Kant's three *Critiques* provides some of the rational principles for imperial expansion. Kant's argument that only cultivated and educated European men have access to the sublime, while non-European subjects are stripped of culture or humanity and relegated to the place of an unrepresentable, irrational other, is an interesting case in point. For it is precisely because of this narrow, European-centred definition of the moral subject that Kant's philosophical narrative could serve to justify the idea of western imperialism as a civilising mission.

THE CLASSIC TEXT AND BRITISH IMPERIALISM: *JANE EYRE*

Significantly, Spivak's reading of Kant is prefigured in 'Three Women's Texts and a Critique of Imperialism' (1985), an essay that was published fourteen years before Spivak's reading of Kant's *Third Critique*. As we saw earlier, this essay shows how the civilising mission of imperialism figures strongly in English literary texts such as Charlotte Brontë's *Jane Eyre* (1847). The main narrative of Brontë's novel may seem to chart the education and development of the white, English bourgeois female protagonist Jane Eyre within the restricted space of the nineteenth-century domestic sphere. Yet at the same time, Jane's narrative of female individualism is achieved at the expense of Bertha Mason, Rochester's first wife, who is taken from her home in the West Indies and confined to Rochester's English household, where she is denied full access to the category of human subject.

As discusssed in Chapter 4, critics such as Sandra Gilbert and Susan Gubar have argued that Bertha Mason embodies Jane's dark double. Spivak insists that such a reading ignores the imperialist sub-text of the novel and denies Bertha's status as a human being in the text. Instead, Spivak asserts that Bertha Mason is 'a figure produced by the axiomatics of imperialism' (Spivak 1985: 247): 'Through Bertha Mason, the white Jamaican Creole, Brontë renders the human/animal frontier as acceptably indeterminate, so that a good greater than the letter of the Law can be broached' (Spivak 1985: 247).

The ethical principle or 'good' that Spivak describes here is registered in Brontë's novel as a 'divine injunction rather than a human motive' to justify imperialism as a civilising mission (Spivak 1985: 247). Spivak further relates this ethical principle to Kant's account of the categorical imperative: a concept that was conceived as 'the universal moral law, given by pure reason' (Spivak 1985: 249). Noting how Kant worded the categorical imperative in religious terms, Spivak argues that the categorical imperative is a 'displacement of Christian ethics from religion to philosophy' (Spivak 1985: 248).

At this point Spivak qualifies her reading with the important disclaimer that the categorical imperative is a philosophical concept, and as such it cannot be linked to the determinate political content of imperialism. This statement is interesting because it anticipates the charges of critics such as Chetan Bhatt, who argues that Spivak's reading of Kant assumes that *The Critique of Judgement* had 'resolved the problem of the relationship between aesthetics and morality' when in actual fact the complex relationship between the good and the beautiful continues to vex Kantian scholars (Bhatt 2001: 41).

Rather than getting side-tracked by the philosophical nuances of Kantian critique, however, Spivak focuses on how the formal subtlety of Kant's philosophy *has been travestied* by the European project of imperialist expansion. For example, Kant's statement that: '"In all creation every thing one chooses and over which one has any power, may be used *merely as means*; man alone, and with him every rational creature, is *an end in himself*", is transformed by the rhetoric of imperialism into: "*make* the heathen into a human so he can be treated as an end in himself"' (Spivak 1985: 248). Spivak thus suggests that European imperialists expressed territorial expansion and conquest as a divine right by appropriating the moral imperatives of western philosophy and religion.

In *Jane Eyre*, the civilising mission of imperialism is explicitly presented in the last section of the text in the terms of a Christian allegory. The hero of this allegory, St John Rivers, is a Christian missionary, who proposes to marry Jane and take her on a pilgrimage to India. Rivers's justification for this project is articulated in the terms of a civilising mission:

> My vocation? My great work? [. . .] My hopes of being numbered in the band who have merged all ambitions in the glorious one of bettering their race – of carrying knowledge into the realms of ignorance – of substituting peace for war – freedom for bondage – religion for superstition – the hope of heaven for the fear of hell?
>
> (Brontë cited in Spivak 1985: 249)

By defining Indian culture as 'a realm of ignorance' where 'superstition' and 'the fear of hell' prevail, Rivers is thus able to justify his 'great work' through the moral imperative of a soul-making enterprise. Although Spivak argues that the last section of the text is tangential to the main narrative, this 'tangent narrative' or textual margin is fundamental to the 'territorial and subject constituting project' of imperialism (Spivak 1985: 249).

As I suggested at the beginning of this chapter, Spivak's approach to reading colonial discourse – in nineteenth-century British literature or eighteenth-century German philosophy – may display some affinities with the colonial discourse analysis of Edward Said. Yet in contrast to Said's totalising model of colonialism, Spivak has also demonstrated the rhetorical and political agency of postcolonial literary texts to question and challenge the authority of colonial master narratives.

POSTCOLONIAL REWRITING

In 'Three Women's Texts and a Critique of Imperialism' (1985) Spivak examines the rhetorical agency of one such postcolonial narrative in Jean

Rhys's novel *Wide Sargasso Sea* (1965). By writing part of the text from the point of view of Bertha Mason, Rhys offers a crucial and situated counterpoint to Rochester's colonial narrative in *Jane Eyre*. In contrast to the narrative of *Jane Eyre*, the main events of *Wide Sargasso Sea* are located in Jamaica, during the time of the emancipation from colonial slavery in the early nineteenth century. What is more, Rhys explicitly challenges the representation of Bertha Mason as a monstrous, inhuman figure in *Jane Eyre* by showing how Antoinette, a white Creole child, is violently renamed as Bertha Mason by Rochester in the second part of the text. As Spivak comments, 'In the figure of Antoinette, whom in *Wide Sargasso Sea* Rochester violently re-names Bertha, Rhys suggests that so intimate a thing as personal identity might be determined by the politics of imperialism' (Spivak 1985: 250).

Antoinette's position as a vocal critic of imperialism is certainly compromised later in *Wide Sargasso Sea* by her circumscribed position as a legal object within the patriarchal terms of the marriage to Rochester. Yet as Spivak points out, Rhys's rewriting of Bertha as Antoinette 'keeps Bertha's humanity, indeed her sanity as a critic of imperialism intact' (Spivak 1985: 249).

Rhys powerfully articulates this criticism of imperialism, in a scene that rewrites the events leading up to the fire at Thornfield Hall in *Jane Eyre*. In this scene Antoinette recounts her experience of the journey from the West Indies to England; and how her cultural identity is denied when Rochester 'wouldn't call me Antoinette, and I saw Antoinette drifting out of the window, with her scents, her pretty clothes and her looking glass' (Rhys 1997: 117). Antoinette's experience of cultural non-being is exacerbated at Thornfield Hall, where she asks, 'What I am doing in this place and who am I? [. . .] They tell me I am in England, but I don't believe them. We lost our way to England' (Rhys 1997: 117).

In *Jane Eyre* Bertha Mason is presented as a demonic, monstrous fiend who embodies the repression of women in the restricted patriarchal domain of the domestic sphere; in *Wide Sargasso Sea*, Antoinette is portrayed as a sympathetic figure, who is haunted by memories of slavery in Jamaica, and victimised by Rochester's psychological abuse: in his attempt to rename Antoinette as Bertha Mason and to keep her confined to the walls of Thornfield Hall.

Spivak likens Antoinette's experience to the madness of Narcissus in Ovid's *Metamorphoses* 'where Rhys makes Antoinette see her *self* as her

Other, Brontë's Bertha' (Spivak 1985: 250). For Spivak, however, Rhys's rewriting of Brontë's original narrative foregrounds the 'epistemic violence of imperialism' that is embedded in *Jane Eyre* (Spivak 1985: 251). Spivak thus suggests that Rhys's text challenges the dominant assumptions which underpin the operations of imperialism. One of the key assumptions that Spivak identifies in *Jane Eyre* is 'the construction of a self-immolating colonial subject for the glorification of the social mission of the colonies' (Spivak 1985: 251). In other words, by defining the colonial subject as inhuman, heathen or primitive, the British colonial administration was able to justify imperialism as a civilising mission.

Spivak's critical engagement with postcolonial literary texts that seem to challenge or subvert the authority of dominant colonial discourse has been very influential in generating more sophisticated and nuanced accounts of agency in postcolonial texts. Indeed, Spivak's engagement with texts such as *Wide Sargasso Sea* is a particular case in point because it tries to rewrite the colonial narrative embedded in *Jane Eyre* from the point of view of Bertha Mason. But Spivak is also careful not to exaggerate the radical political achievements of such fictional rewritings, as I will go on to suggest later in the chapter. Before doing so, however, I want to look at Spivak's engagement with another postcolonial text which rewrites the colonial narrative in Daniel Defoe's novel *Robinson Crusoe* (1719).

Significantly, postcolonial critics have often cited Defoe's novel *Robinson Crusoe* as one of the original literary texts about English imperialism. In *Culture and Imperialism* (1993), for example, Edward Said argues that it is no accident that Defoe's 'prototypical modern realistic novel is about a European who creates a fiefdom for himself on a distant, non-European island' (Said 1993: xiii). Indeed, for Said '*Robinson Crusoe* is virtually unthinkable without the colonising mission that permits him to create a new world of his own in the distant reaches of the African, Pacific, and Atlantic wilderness' (Said 1993: 75).

In 'Theory in the Margin: Coetzee's *Foe* Reading Defoe's *Crusoe/Roxana*' (1991), Spivak approaches *Robinson Crusoe* from a related, although quite different position by considering how the white, South African novelist J.M. Coetzee rewrites Defoe's novel *Robinson Crusoe* in his 1986 novel *Foe*. Starting with a consideration of Karl Marx's discussion of *Robinson Crusoe* in *Capital Volume One*, Spivak elucidates the exact significance of Defoe's novel to Marx's theory of the commodity.

Following Marx, many commentators have described *Robinson Crusoe* as a cultural representation of early capitalism. For Spivak, however, the reason that Marx invoked *Robinson Crusoe* was merely to illustrate how the value of different forms of productive labour is calculated according to the time taken to complete a particular task. As Marx writes of Defoe's protagonist, Robinson Crusoe:

> Necessity itself compels him to apportion his time accurately between his different kinds of work. Whether one kind occupies a greater space in his general activity than another depends upon the difficulties, greater or less as the case may be, to be overcome in attaining the useful effect aimed at. This our friend Robinson soon learns by experience, and having rescued a watch, ledger, and pen and ink from the wreck, commences, like a true-born Briton, to keep a set of books. His stock-book contains a list of the objects of utility that belong to him, of the operations necessary for their production; and lastly for the labour time that definite quantities of those objects have, on average, cost him.
>
> (Marx 1977: 439)

By invoking this passage from *Capital*, Spivak emphasises that 'Time, rather than money, is the general equivalent that expresses [the proto-capitalist form of] production' in *Robinson Crusoe* (Spivak 1991: 161).

This reading of *Robinson Crusoe* via Marx may seem to be discontinuous with colonialist readings of the novel, but it is not entirely unrelated. For Spivak's reading echoes her own critical engagement with Marx's economic writings on value and labour, and the question of whether Marx overlooked the importance of imperial conquest to the expansion of European capitalism (see Chapter 4, p. 93). By invoking Marx's reading of *Robinson Crusoe*, Spivak thus suggests that Marx subordinated questions about space and imperialism to the historical narrative of European capitalism and the calculation of labour in that European narrative.

Indeed, this point is made more explicit in Spivak's reading of J.M. Coetzee's novel *Foe*: '*Foe* is more about spacing and displacement than about the timing of history and labour' (Spivak 1991: 161). By emphasising the geographical location of *Robinson Crusoe*, Coetzee foregrounds the imperialist determinants that form the backdrop of Defoe's narrative. Like Jean Rhys's rewriting of Rochester's colonialist narrative in *Jane Eyre*, Coetzee rewrites *Robinson Crusoe* in order to challenge the authority of Crusoe's colonial narrative.

This rewriting is accomplished in part by substituting a female narrator, Susan Barton, for Defoe's male narrator. As Spivak notes, 'Coetzee's focus is on gender and empire, rather than the story of capital [. . .] The narrator of *Foe* is an Englishwoman named Susan Barton, who wants to "father" her story into history, with Mr Foe's help' (Spivak 1991: 162). But perhaps one of the most obvious instances of post-colonial rewriting in Coetzee's novel is Susan Barton's attempt to give a voice to Friday. In *Robinson Crusoe*, Robinson carries out the civilising mission of the European imperialist by teaching Friday to speak English. In doing so, Defoe recalls a scene in Shakespeare's play *The Tempest*, where Prospero's daughter, Miranda, teaches the native character Caliban to speak English.

In Coetzee's *Foe*, however, the violence of colonial education, which is effaced in these earlier texts, is foregrounded as Friday is revealed to have had his tongue removed by slave traders. Susan Barton tries to remedy this muteness by finding a 'means of giving voice to Friday' (Coetzee cited in Spivak 1991: 169). At first, Barton encourages Friday to 'explain the origin of his loss through a few pictures' (Spivak 1991: 168). Through a process of trial and error, Susan Barton gradually recognises the futility of trying to represent Friday's traumatic experience in pictures. As Spivak comments: 'The unrepeatability of the unique event can only be repeated imperfectly' (Spivak 1991: 168). Finally, Susan Barton grows impatient with her failure and reluctantly attempts to teach Friday how to write.

Spivak underlines the fact that one of the words that Susan Barton teaches Friday is 'Africa'. For Spivak the word Africa is a catachresis, or an improper word, because it was historically imposed on a continent by a European colonial power: '*Africa* is only a time-bound naming; like all proper names it is a mark with an arbitrary connection to its referent' (Spivak 1991: 170). By teaching Friday the word Africa, Susan thus attempts to give Friday the language to assert national independence and thereby to challenge Defoe's original colonial narrative. Yet during the course of the writing lesson, Friday proceeds to draw 'walking eyes' on the writing slate handed to him by Susan Barton: 'Friday filled his slate with open eyes, each set upon a human foot: row upon row of eyes: walking eyes' (cited in Spivak 1991: 171). When Susan Barton demands that Friday show her the slate, Friday immediately erases the drawing. This event leads Susan Barton to conclude that the writing lesson is pointless, an opinion which is borne out by her rhetorical question, 'How can Friday know what freedom means when he barely knows his own name?' (cited in Spivak 1991: 171).

For Spivak, however, the failure of Barton's writing lesson provides an instructive reading lesson for readers of postcolonial texts. Rather than a passive victim of colonial history, Spivak argues that Friday is an 'agent of withholding in the text' who refuses to yield an authentic native voice (Spivak 1991: 172). Indeed for Spivak, there is no rhetorical space available to Friday in Susan Barton's benevolent anti-colonial narrative. Friday's refusal to speak could thus be seen to push against the agendas of nationalism and identity, which Susan Barton employs in the attempt to emancipate Friday and to restore his voice.

Spivak's reading of Coetzee's *Foe* is important because it reveals how Spivak's critical thinking has increasingly sought to challenge the exaggerated political claims that are sometimes made on behalf of postcolonial texts. Rather than simply rewriting *Robinson Crusoe* from the point of view of Friday, for example, Spivak suggests that Friday's agency lies in his refusal to be represented. By doing so, Spivak emphasises that Coetzee draws attention to the limitations of postcolonial representation as an effective vehicle for political change.

Indeed, Spivak has increasingly emphasised how the term '*postcolonial*' can be misleading if it is taken to signify a straightforward historical break with the political, cultural and economic legacy of colonialism. As Spivak writes in *A Critique of Postcolonial Reason*, 'Colonial Discourse studies, when they concentrate only on the representation of the colonized or the matter of the colonies, can sometimes serve the production of current neo-colonial knowledge by placing colonialism/imperialism securely in the past' (Spivak 1999: 1). Such an argument is echoed in Leela Gandhi's assertion that postcolonialism is 'a disciplinary project devoted to the academic task of revisiting, remembering and, crucially, interrogating the colonial past' (Gandhi 1998: 4).

As I have suggested, Spivak's engagement with postcolonial texts is motivated in part by a desire to challenge the totalising system of colonial discourse by focusing on instances of subaltern agency or resistance. In this respect, Spivak's reading of postcolonial literary texts can be seen to echo the political imperatives of earlier anti-colonial thinkers and writers such as Chinua Achebe (1930–), Frantz Fanon (1925–61), and Ngũgĩ wa Thiong 'o' (1938–) to challenge the authority of European imperialism and its cultural texts. Yet Spivak is also relentlessly critical of the political promises of Third World nationalism and decolonisation, especially from the perspective of subaltern women and the underclass.

This criticism of postcolonial nationalism is informed by the historical thought of Subaltern Studies scholars such as Partha Chatterjee, who argues that nationalism is a 'derivative discourse' that was inherited from European political ideas via the civilising mission of colonialism. Following Chatterjee, Spivak argues that postcolonial nationalism is divided between the state political programmes of ruling governmental elites and the popular struggles of the people who are often ignored by these dominant political programmes:

> If nationalism is the *only* discourse credited with emancipatory possibilities in the imperialist theatre, then one must ignore the innumerable examples of resistance throughout the imperialist and pre-imperialist centuries, often suppressed by those very forces of nationalism which would be instrumental in changing the geopolitical conjuncture from territorial imperialism to neo-colonialism.
>
> (Spivak 1987: 245)

If dominant history writes the popular struggles and peasant rebellions out of national liberation movements, however, Spivak suggests that literature can provide a rhetorical space for sublatern groups to re-articulate the suppressed histories of popular struggles.

RE-IMAGINING HISTORY: MAHASWETA DEVI AND THE LITERARY HISTORIES OF SUBALTERN WOMEN

It is in the translations and commentaries on the Bengali-language writer Mahasweta Devi that Spivak has perhaps done more than any other literary critic to articulate the histories and struggles of subaltern women with a political commitment that is always tempered by an acute awareness of the ethical limitations of such a project.

As mentioned briefly in previous chapters, one example of this is seen in 'A Literary Representation of the Subaltern', where Spivak considers how Mahasweta Devi's story 'Stanadayini' ('Breast Giver') challenges the truth claims of elite historical discourse in India by narrating the story of national independence from the point of view of a subaltern woman. In Mahasweta Devi's authorial commentary on the story, the tragic narrative of Jashoda, a subaltern woman, who is forced into servile labour as a mother to nurse the children of a wealthy Brahmin family, is 'a parable of decolonization' (Spivak 1987: 244). For Devi, the maternal body of Jashoda stands as a metaphor for the national body politic after decolonisation: 'Like the protagonist Jashoda, India is a mother by hire. All classes of people, the post-war rich, the ideologues, the indigenous bureaucracy, the diasporics, the people who are sworn to protect the new state, abuse and exploit her' (Spivak 1987: 244).

Such a reading of 'Stanadayini' certainly emphasises how a gendered discourse has been invoked to represent the Indian nation state to its citizenry. Indeed, Devi's reading locates Jashoda's narrative in relation to the metaphor of Mother India that was prevalent during the campaign of non-violent, passive resistance against the British Empire led by Gandhi. This metaphor of Mother India has its roots in nineteenth-century anti-colonial resistance movements, where powerful feminine figures from Hindu mythology like Kali, Sita, Draupadi and Savatri were mobilised to help define a coherent sense of Indian nationhood. As Ketu Katrak (1992) argues, Gandhi extended the metaphor of Mother India in nationalist discourse to mobilise the active support of women in public demonstrations of passive resistance against the British. Yet as Katrak further emphasises, Gandhi's political mobilisation of women through a gendered discourse of nationalism during the anti-colonial resistance movement did not lead to women's political emancipation. Rather, the political mobilisation of women was subordinated to the more immediate goal of national independence. When national independence was finally achieved in 1947, however, women's rights were disregarded, and the gendered discourse of nationalism was revealed to contain women within the traditional gender role of motherhood and unwaged domestic worker.

For Spivak, Devi's reading of the story as an allegory of nationalism troublingly ignores the lower-class position of subaltern women such as Jashoda. Against Devi's authorial commentary on the story, Spivak argues that 'Stanadayini' highlights the particular social oppression of subaltern women in the context of postcolonial nationalism. Drawing on the critical vocabulary of Marxist feminism, Spivak demonstrates how Jashoda's reproductive body becomes a site of economic exploitation in the text: 'The protagonist subaltern Jashoda, [whose] husband [was] crippled by the youngest son of a wealthy household [after the husband tries to rob the household], becomes a wet-nurse for them. Her repeated gestation and lactation support her husband and family. By the logic of the production of value, they are both means of production' (Spivak 1987: 247).

By invoking the themes of Marxist feminism, Spivak argues that Jashoda problematises the male-centred definition of the working-class subject that underwrites classic European Marxism. In the classic Marxist theory of labour, for example, there is a sexual division of labour between productive labour (masculine) and reproductive labour (feminine) which is based on an essentialist notion of sexual difference. This sexual division of labour has conventionally devalued and ignored the material specificity of women's domestic work, including childbirth and mothering, because these forms of work do not directly produce exchange value or money.

In 'Stanadayini', however, the protagonist Jashoda illustrates how a subaltern woman's reproductive body is employed to produce economic value. As Spivak argues, Jashoda's sale of her maternal body to the household of a wealthy Brahmin family to support her own family effectively reverses this traditional sexual division of labour between men and women. Of course this is not to suggest that Jashoda is simply empowered because she is the sole breadwinner in the household, or that Devi's story poetically resolves some of the theoretical contradictions that have vexed western Marxist feminism for more than three decades. Rather, Spivak argues that Jashoda's employment as a professional mother crucially 'invokes the singularity of the gendered subaltern' (Spivak 1987: 252). By doing so, '"Stanadayini" calls into question that aspect of Western Marxist feminism which, from the point of view of work, trivializes the theory of value and, from the point of view of mothering as work, ignores the mother as subject' (Spivak 1987: 258).

Spivak's reading and translation of 'Breast Giver' is very persuasive, although it is not above criticism. In an essay on Spivak's textual commentaries and translations of Mahasweta Devi's fiction, Minoli Salgado (2000) identifies several discrepancies between Devi's original stories and Spivak's translations of these stories. In particular, Salgado notes how Spivak's italicisation of English words in Devi's original text work to 'dramatize the effects of state domination' (Salgado 2000: 134). By doing so, Salgado contends that Spivak exaggerates the 'contestational and oppositional nature of Mahasweta's work' (Salgado 2000:

135). Indeed, Spivak's 'claim that Mahasweta's work punctures nationalist discourse' would seem to contradict Mahasweta's call 'for the tribal people's insertion into the Indian mainstream' (Salgado 2000: 135).

What is at stake in Salgado's criticism of Spivak's translation and interpretation of Mahasweta Devi's writing is a broader argument that Spivak is helping to commodify Mahasweta Devi's texts for an international market by inserting the texts into a western theoretical discourse which has no connection or relationship to the people or culture depicted in Devi's fiction. This is certainly a limitation with Spivak's translations of Mahasweta Devi, although, to be fair, Spivak does acknowledge this difficulty at the forefront of her translations:

> The ravenous hunger for Third World literary texts in English translation is part of the benevolence and part of the problem [. . .] by translating this text ['Stanadayini'] I am contributing to both.
>
> (Spivak 1987: 253)

To alleviate this difficulty, Spivak develops an ethics of reading which is more sensitive to the social location of subaltern women. Against the charges of theoretical difficulty made by critics such as Minoli Salgado (2000) and Benita Parry (1987), Spivak argues that such charges are based on a critical position 'which predicates the possibility of knowledge on identity' (Spivak 1987: 254). Spivak is certainly sceptical about the political benefits to be gained from benevolent western radicals speaking for postcolonial subjects. As Spivak writes, 'It is when *only* the [dominant] groups theorize that the situation becomes intolerable' (Spivak 1987: 253).

Spivak does not rule out the possibility of an alliance between dominant readers and the texts of subalternity altogether, but reformulates this relation as an ethical relation to the other: 'knowledge is made possible and is sustained by irreducible difference, not identity' (Spivak 1987: 254). Such an argument is based on Jacques Derrida's notion of ethics as a responsibility of the (western) self towards the (non-western) other. John Hill offers a lucid commentary on the wider application of Derrida's ethical thought to postcolonial studies in an essay on the Irish director Neil Jordan's film *The Crying Game*. Hill writes that:

> [Derrida] emphasises that the words 'respond' and 'responsibility' have the same root. Thus *answering* to the other is in itself a recognition of the

responsibility you have towards the other. The obligation the other's responsibility puts on you is the obligation to *respond*, in a strange kind of relationship
which precedes relationship [. . .] indicating that in the having to listen, in the
having to answer to the other, a relationship of responsibility is already in place,
prior to any engagement.

(Hill 1998: 98–9)

Derrida's paradoxical understanding of ethics as a relationship of
responsibility which is prior to any inter-subjective engagement
between the Self and the Other also informs Spivak's ethics of reading
postcolonial literary texts. One of the clearest examples of this ethical
relation is seen in a revised version of 'Three Women's Texts and a
Critique of Imperialism' which compares the evocation of sympathy for
the Other in Mary Shelley's *Frankenstein* (1818) and Mahasweta Devi's
'Pterodactyl' (1995). For Spivak, Mary Shelley's sympathetic representation of the monster-as-colonial-subject is paralleled by Devi's
evocation of the reader's (ethical) response to the beleagured tribal
communities which are threatened with extinction in the postcolonial
world of the story. However, Spivak adds that there is no guarantee that
the reader's response will lead to an ethical relation to the singularity
of the Other.

What is more, Spivak's concern to develop an ethical relation with
the subaltern through reading also questions the limits of political representation as a critical strategy. Such a reading is contrary to Mahasweta
Devi's argument that her fiction 'posits the need for the tribal people's
insertion into the Indian mainstream' (Devi cited in Salgado 2000: 135).
For Spivak this reading is based on a naive understanding of political
representation, which falsely assumes that literary representation
will necessarily lead to the political representation of tribal subaltern
groups. Instead, Spivak emphasises that Devi's fiction formally articulates the structural barriers of class, culture, language and literacy that
prevent tribal groups from participating in the parliamentary democracy of post-independence India.

In Mahasweta Devi's story 'Douloti the Bountiful', for example, the
limits of democracy are foregrounded in an exchange between the washerwoman Rajbi and the Gandhian prophet Sadhuji. In this dialogue, the
narrator foregrounds the split between the everyday lives of tribal
women and the gendered discourse of the nation state.

You are not untouchable. You, me, Munabar Chandela, are offspring of the same mother.

Hearing all this the washerwoman Rajbi said, 'How can that be, Sadhuji [Mr Holy Man]?'

– Yes, sister, quite true.

– Why, what happened?

– We are all offspring of the same mother.

– No Sadhuji, untrue, untrue.

– Why?

– If the offspring of the same mother, we are all brothers and sisters, yes?

– Should be.

– But Munabar doesn't know that. Munabar's children in my room, Munabar's children in Mukami Dusadin's place as well, and all these boys are bonded labor. Tell me how this can be.

– Sister, not that kind of mother, Mother India.

– Who is that?

– Our country, India.

– This is our country?

– Of course.

– Oh Sadhuji, my place is Seora village. What do you call a country? I know *tahsil* [a pre-independence revenue collecting unit], I know station, I don't know country. India is not the country.

– Hey, you are all independent India's free people, do you understand?

– No, Sadhuji.

(Devi 1995: 41)

Sadhuji's insistence that Rajbi is one of the 'offspring' of Mother India and not an untouchable falls on deaf ears. For Rajbi, the democratic rhetoric of independent India is meaningless because it has no relationship to the material reality of her everyday life. As Spivak points out, the 'rituals' of democracy seem 'absurd' to those people who continue to be brutally exploited by India's class-caste system. Like the bond-slaves' misunderstanding of the voting booths and the Census in 'Douloti the Bountiful', Sadhuji's confusion about the rhetoric of decolonisation and national liberation emphasises the failure of national independence to radically change the lives of tribal subaltern communities.

More urgently, Spivak's readings and translations of Mahasweta Devi's short fiction illustrate how the violence of decolonisation and national liberation is often brutally inscribed on the material bodies of subaltern women. In 'Stanadayini', the nationalist myth of Mother India is contrasted with the grotesque description of Jashoda's cancerous breast, which 'bursts and becomes like the *crater* of a volcano' after Jashoda breast feeds several children in an upper-class household. For Spivak, Jashoda's cancerous breast embodies the specific material 'oppression of the gendered subaltern' (Spivak 1987: 267).

WOMEN'S BODIES IN REVOLT

The tragic and gruesome denouement of 'Stanadayini' is echoed in Devi's story, 'Douloti the Bountiful'. In the final section of the story, we are presented with the spectacle of Douloti's corpse, which is 'putrefied with venereal disease' after Douloti is sold into bonded labour as a prostitute to pay off her father's debts. Significantly, the event of Douloti's death takes place on a political map of India, which is drawn in clay on the ground by a local village schoolmaster the previous night. When the schoolmaster returns the following day to teach his class about the political geography of India, both schoolmaster and students are confronted with the following spectacle:

> Filling the entire Indian peninsula from the oceans to the Himalayas, here lies bonded labor spreadeagled, kamiya-whore Douloti Nagesia's tormented corpse, putrefied with venereal disease, having vomited up all the blood in her desiccated lungs.
>
> (Devi cited in Parker *et al.* 1992: 112)

The appearance of Douloti's corpse on a map of India powerfully illustrates how the act of political independence from the British Empire is founded on the continued social and political oppression of subaltern women. As Spivak asserts: 'The space *displaced* from the empire-nation negotiation now comes to inhabit and appropriate the national map, and makes the agenda of nationalism impossible' (Spivak in Parker *et al.* 1992: 113). In other words, Douloti's brutalised corpse marks the limits of decolonisation in post-independence India and the failure of political independence to effectively change the class and gender inequalities in Indian society.

For Spivak, one of the important questions that the fiction of Mahasweta Devi raises is whether subaltern women such as Douloti and Jashoda have any political agency or voice in the nation state. Certainly,

Devi's fiction presents the reader with a picture of the subaltern woman's body literally revolting against the postcolonial state. But these acts of bodily resistance and revolt are clearly not a sign of *intentional* political struggle. For the exploited and abused bodies of Jashoda and Douloti stand as a painful reminder of the class and gender inequalities that continue to divide India, despite the emancipatory promises made by the ruling political elite in the name of decolonisation and democracy.

This question of subaltern women's political agency is further explored in Mahasweta Devi's short story, 'Draupadi', which has also been translated into English by Spivak. The story is set in a Northern region of West Bengal during the time of a rural-based peasant rebellion against economic and political oppression by landowners and the government in the late 1960s. The narrative recounts the events leading up to the capture and subsequent torture of one of the peasant insurgents by the state military forces, a woman named Draupadi or Dopdi Mejhen.

As Spivak notes in the 'Translator's Foreword' to 'Draupadi', the first part of the story is narrated from the point of view of Senanayak, the army chief who hunts the leaders of the Naxalite rebellion. In order to catch the leaders of the peasant rebellion, Senanayak tries to understand the political motivation of the insurgents by reading left-wing paperbacks and literature. For Spivak, Senanayak's avaricious intellectual pursuit is not dissimilar to 'the First-World scholar in search of the Third World' (Spivak 1987: 179). Indeed, for Spivak, Senanayak's futile attempt to translate Dopdi's song later in the story could be seen to mirror the 'First World' reader's desire to know the subaltern by interpreting Devi's story:

Although we are told of specialists, the meaning of Dopdi's song remains undisclosed in the text. The educated Bengali does not know the languages of the tribes, and no political coercion obliges him to 'know' it. What one might falsely think of as a political privilege – knowing English properly – stands in the way of a deconstructive practice of language – using it 'correctly' through a political displacement, or operating the language of the other side.

(Spivak 1987: 186)

As Spivak points out, the 'privilege' of 'knowing English properly' prevents both Senanayak and the First World reader from translating

Draupadi's song. In this respect, Draupadi could be seen as a textual enigma, whose agency lies in the refusal to confess her meaning and story to the reader.

The story also raises questions about Draupadi's political agency through its rewriting of the ancient Indian epic the *Mahabharata*. In the original ancient epic, Draupadi is 'married to the five sons of the impotent Pandu' and is 'used to demonstrate male glory' (Spivak 1987: 183). Since Draupadi is married to several husbands, an act which is contrary to the law of the scriptures, Draupadi is 'designated a prostitute' (cited in Spivak 1987: 183). In the terms of the scriptures, this designation permits male chiefs to bring her 'clothed or unclothed, into the assembly' (Spivak 1987: 183). During a scene wherein Draupadi's eldest husband loses his wife as a stake in a game of dice, the enemy chief 'begins to pull at Draupadi's *sari*' (183). What follows is perceived to be 'one of Krishna's miracles' (183). As Spivak writes:

> The enemy chief begins to pull at Draupadi's *sari*. Draupadi silently prays to the incarnate Krishna. The Idea of Sustaining Law (Dharma) materializes itself as clothing, and as the king pulls and pulls at her *sari*, there seems to more and more of it. Draupadi is infinitely clothed and cannot be publically stripped.
>
> (Spivak 1987: 183)

In the *Mahabharata*, Draupadi's dignity and honour are thus preserved by the divine intervention of the male Hindu God, Krishna.

Mahasweta Devi rewrites this scene from the *Mahabharata* by having Draupadi 'remain publically naked at her own insistence' (Spivak 1987: 184). Following orders from Senanayak, Dopdi is violently raped by military guards. In defiance of this violent act, Dopdi subsequently confronts Senanayak with the bloody spectacle of her tortured and ravaged body:

> Draupadi stands before him, naked. Thigh and pubic hair matted with dry blood. Two breasts, two wounds.
>
> What is this? He is about to bark.
>
> Draupadi comes closer. Stands with her hand on her hip, laughs and says, The object of your search, Dopdi Mejhen. You asked them to make me up, don't you want to see how they made me?
>
> (cited in Spivak 1987: 196)

In spite of her violent physical and sexual torture by the military, Draupadi's refusal to be clothed stands as an unequivocal sign of political resistance and agency. Indeed, the violent spectacle of Draupadi's ravaged body threatens the authority of the patriarchal state, which is personified by Senanayak. As the narrator asserts, 'Draupadi pushes Senanayak with her two mangled breasts, and for the first time Senanayak is afraid to stand before an unarmed *target*, terribly afraid' (cited in Spivak 1987: 196). This threat to patriarchal authority is reiterated in Draupadi's interrogation of her torturers: 'What's the use of clothes? You can strip me, but how can you clothe me again? Are you a man?' (cited in Spivak 1987: 196).

For Spivak, Draupadi's questions effectively reverse the linguistic subject positions of the interrogator and the interrogated, and so work to challenge the authority of the ruling elite. Similarly, Draupadi's imperative to Senanayak to 'counter' her further undermines the secure opposition between the active subject of interrogation and the passive object of torture. Spivak notes that Draupadi's use of the word 'counter' 'is an abbreviation for "killed by police in an encounter," the code description for death by police torture' (Spivak 1987: 186). Yet, Draupadi's use of the verb counter rather than encounter is closer to the '"proper" English usage' (Spivak 1987: 186).

For Spivak this 'correct' use of the English language is significant because Draupadi would have no knowledge of the English language as a rural, tribal person with only basic knowledge of spoken Bengali: 'Dopdi does not understand English, but she understands this formula and the word' (Spivak 1987: 186). Draupadi's correct understanding of the English word 'counter' is thus derived from a political consciousness of state violence and oppression from the standpoint of a tribal, subaltern woman, rather than a privileged education in English semantics. For this reason, Spivak argues that Draupadi's use of the imperative 'counter me' is a powerful 'deconstructive practice of language', a practice that uses language '"correctly" through a political displacement, or operat[es] the language of the other side' (Spivak 1987: 186).

As I have suggested, Spivak's translations and commentaries on Mahasweta Devi's fiction have done much to articulate the histories of tribal subaltern women. Spivak is certainly very conscious of the political risks involved in translating Devi's fiction for a largely western readership. One of the dangers with Spivak's translations is that the narratives could be taken out of context to represent a tragic stereotype of postcolonial victimhood.

By employing the critical tools of deconstruction, however, Spivak resists the temptation to represent the fictional subaltern characters in Mahasweta Devi's writing as transparent objects of knowledge for western-trained intellectuals. Instead, Spivak traces the linguistic and rhetorical nuances in Devi's texts where tribal, subaltern women characters like Jashoda, Draupadi or Douloti articulate an embodied knowledge that cannot be accounted for in the dominant terms of western knowledge and representation.

SUMMARY

- Spivak's critical engagement with classic nineteenth-century English literary texts has demonstrated how the institution of English literary studies disseminated the idea of English imperialism. In this respect her work has contributed much to the study of literature as a colonial discourse.

- Spivak is most famous for her critical engagements with postcolonial literature as a counter-discourse that can challenge the authority of colonial master narratives in classic English literary texts such as Charlotte Brontë's *Jane Eyre* and Daniel Defoe's *Robinson Crusoe*.

- However, Spivak is increasingly sceptical of the radical potential of *all* postcolonial fiction to effectively challenge the condition of subaltern groups living under contemporary conditions of global exploitation.

- Nevertheless, Spivak's translations and commentaries on the Bengali-language writer and activist Mahasweta Devi emphasise the importance of Devi's literary and activist writing to articulate the unwritten histories of tribal, subaltern women and to at least begin to imagine an alternative to contemporary social, political and economic oppression.

AFTER SPIVAK

In 1999 Spivak's long awaited book *A Critique of Postcolonial Reason: Towards a History of the Vanishing Present* was published by Harvard University Press. This book is significant for many reasons, not least because it signals Spivak's rejection of the label 'postcolonial' which had previously been applied to her work. What is more, the book contains a revised version of 'Can the Subaltern Speak?'; an ingenious reading of the German philosophers Immanuel Kant, G.W.F. Hegel and Karl Marx as colonial discourse theorists before the letter; and a sustained critique of the cultural and economic effects of globalisation. These ambitious projects collectively demonstrate the continued importance and influence of Spivak's intellectual work. For one of Spivak's most important and valuable contributions to contemporary critical theory and public intellectual culture is her relentless ability to revise and rework earlier concepts and debates about postcolonialism, or the cultural, political and economic legacy of colonialism, in a way that is directly related to the contemporary conditions of global capitalism.

A Critique of Postcolonial Reason was also the occasion for a conference panel on Spivak's thought at the twenty-fourth annual conference of the International Association of Literature and Philosophy (2000) held in Stony Brook, New York State. This conference panel included papers by figures such as the legal theorist Drucilla Cornell and the literary theorist Thomas Keenan, and covered topics such as Spivak's reading of

Immanuel Kant's *Third Critique* and the question of human rights in Spivak's thought.

Spivak's intellectual influence is not exclusively confined to an academic audience, however. In their introduction to *The Spivak Reader* (1996), Donna Landry and Gerald Maclean describe how Spivak was embraced by a group of African American women from the Detroit community after giving a lecture at the Detroit Arts Centre: 'For these women, Spivak's feminist critique of the links between racism and capitalism had been crucial for their intellectual development. They embraced her as a profoundly political sister, not as an inaccessible academic' (cited in Spivak 1996: 3). Spivak has also gained increasing recognition and respect in Indian public culture for her critical work and translations of Mahasweta Devi (which have received critical praise in journals such as *Economic and Political Weekly*). From these examples, one can see that Spivak's thought has gained a wide international public audience, despite the accusations of elitism and difficulty that have been made by her more hostile critics.

THE FUTURE OF POSTCOLONIAL THEORY

Spivak's international reputation as a postcolonial critic was sealed by the publication in 1990 of *The Post-Colonial Critic*, a collection of interviews and dialogues with Spivak, edited by Sarah Harasym. Indeed, the publication of this book led the literary critic Sangeeta Ray to argue that Spivak has been commodified and marketed as '*the* postcolonial critic in the intellectual marketplace' (Ray 1992: 191). The growing importance and popularity of Spivak's thought has also led Robert Young (1995) to declare Spivak a member of a Holy Trinity of postcolonial critics that also includes Homi Bhabha and Edward Said. The commodification of postcolonial theory in general and Spivak's thought in particular has been harshly criticised by Arif Dirlik in 'The Postcolonial Aura: Third World Criticism in the Age of Global Capitalism' (1994). In Dirlik's view, the success of Spivak's critical thinking in the US academy is symptomatic of how postcolonial intellectuals are 'beneficiaries' rather than 'victims' of global capitalism (Dirlik 1994: 353). Along with Edward Said and Homi Bhabha, Dirlik contends that Spivak has contributed to a postcolonial theory that diverts attention away from global capitalism by focusing on questions of culture (Dirlik 1994: 347).

In what could be read as a response to Dirlik's criticism, Spivak has recently rejected the label of postcolonial critic, on the grounds that the term has lost its explanatory power. One of the reasons for this is that 'Colonial Discourse studies [. . .] can sometimes serve the production of current neocolonial knowledge by placing colonialism/imperialism securely in the past' (Spivak 1999: 1). More importantly, Spivak has explicitly criticised the privileged position of postcolonial intellectuals in the western academy because it can be mistaken for the real political and economic oppression suffered by disenfranchised, subaltern populations in the 'Third World'. Instead of assuming this mistaken identity, Spivak has developed a self-conscious criticism of the class-privileges enjoyed by diasporic intellectuals living in North America. This aspect of Spivak's thought has generated an important critical interest in the cultural histories of new immigrants in North America, and includes work such as Lisa Lowe's *Immigrant Acts* (1997), Rey Chow's *Writing Diaspora* (1993) and *Ethics After Idealism* (1998), and Amitava Kumar's *Passport Photos* (2000). Again, this restless process of self-criticism and revision demonstrates the importance of Spivak's earlier postcolonial thought, and its continued relevance to the contemporary world, even as the original terms of postcolonial theory are reworked to reflect the conditions of contemporary global capitalism.

MARXIST THOUGHT AFTER SPIVAK

Spivak's rethinking of Marx has had a profound impact on the critical analysis of global capitalism and its constitutive inequalities. The political economist Saskia Sassen has praised 'the intricate labyrinth' that Spivak constructs through 'transnational cultural studies' (Spivak 1999: blurb), while in *Oscillate Wildly* (1999), the Marxist literary critic Peter Hitchcock cites Spivak as one of the few intellectuals of our time to rethink the body 'within the space of contemporary transnational capitalism' (Hitchcock 1999: 15).

Spivak's readings of Marx via Derrida have further influenced Thomas Keenan's rhetorical reading of Marx's *Capital Volume One* in *Fables of Responsibility* (1997), Noel Castree's lucid re-articulation of Marx's labour theory of value 'Invisible Leviathan' (1996/7), and have also helped to clarify Jacques Derrida's recent engagement with Marx in *Specters of Marx* (1994). Surprisingly, however, Derrida's response to Spivak's reading of Derrida and Marx has been less than generous. In

'Marx and Sons' (1999) Derrida accuses Spivak of a 'jealous posses-
siveness' that pathetically claims to 'appropriate' the 'textual inherit-
ance' of Marx (Derrida 1999: 222). Despite this rebuttal, Spivak's main
objection that Derrida has failed to address Marx's main argument about
industrial capitalism in *Capital Volume Two* remains unanswered.

SPIVAK AND TRANSNATIONAL FEMINISM

Another significant political impact that Spivak's work has had is in the
area of women's studies and feminist theory. In *Bodies That Matter*
(1993), Judith Butler invokes Spivak's discussion of strategic essentialism to elaborate a theory of gender performativity. Spivak's criticism
of western feminism's complicity with imperialism has also been taken
up by the Canadian feminist critic Julia Emberley in *Thresholds of
Difference* (1993), Laura Donaldson in *Decolonizing Feminisms* (1992) and
the feminist ethnographer Kamala Visweswaran in *Fictions of Feminist
Ethnography* (1994).

In 'French Feminism Revisited' and 'Feminism and Deconstruction
Again: Negotiations', Spivak has revised her earlier critiques of French
feminism to focus instead on the political, historical and theoretical
rethinking of 'recognizably "French" feminisms' (Spivak 1993: 141) in
the fiction and critical writing of the Algerian feminist writer Assia
Djebar.

Furthermore, Spivak has been increasingly vocal in her criticism of
global development policies which focus on women in the 'Third
World'. In a response to the United Nations Conference on Women in
Beijing in 1995, Spivak emphasised how women living in the southern
hemisphere bear the brunt of global economic exploitation today, yet
are not represented in the global theatre of international politics. In
short, the rhetoric of women's rights in the United Nations paradoxically overlooks the 'poorest women of the South': the very women
whom the United Nations are claiming to represent. More recently, in
'Claiming Transformation' (2000) Spivak has cautioned against the
rhetoric of United Nations declarations on women's rights, which seem
to confuse access to global telecommunications and the right to bear
credit with 'Third World' women's political empowerment as such.
The crucial problem with this claim to represent the political interests
of 'Third World' women is that there is no attempt to change the infra-
structural conditions which maintain the economic impoverishment of

these rural-based women. The feminist spin of development policies and United Nations rhetoric thus appears empty and cynical in the face of current global inequalities between educated professional women in northern developed industrial nations and subaltern women in 'developing' nations in the south.

Spivak's criticism of economic development policies which target women has highlighted the urgent need for a transnational perspective in feminist thought. In a collection of essays, entitled *Feminist Genealogies, Colonial Legacies, Democratic Futures* (1997), M. Jacqui Alexander and Chandra Talpade Mohanty criticise the western feminist dream of a global sisterhood. For Alexander and Mohanty, this idea of global feminism is unworkable because it defines all women's knowledge in the narrow terms of white, western middle-class women's experiences. In the place of global sisterhood, Alexander and Mohanty propose a more careful and situated approach, which they call transnational feminism. For Alexander and Mohanty, such an approach crucially involves 'a way of thinking about women in similar contexts across the world, in *different* geographical spaces, rather than as all women across the world' (Alexander and Mohanty 1997: xix). This critical endeavour to situate women's social location in a transnational framework of political, economic and social relationships is one of the most important legacies of Spivak's thought.

READING THE SUBALTERN

'Can the Subaltern Speak?' is perhaps the most famous and controversial work that Spivak has produced. Since its publication in 1988, Spivak's essay has generated many critical responses that I can only point towards here. Benita Parry's 'Problems in Current Theories of Colonial Discourse' (1987) offers a scathing critique of Spivak's essay, whereas Robert Young's *White Mythologies* (1990) focuses on *sati* as the 'place of woman's disappearance [. . .] an *aporia*, a blind-spot where understanding and knowledge is blocked' (Young 1990: 164). Asha Varadharajan's *Exotic Parodies* (1995) attempts to redeem the urgent political claims that Spivak makes in 'Can the Subaltern Speak?' via the critical theory of Theodor Adorno, while in *Postcolonial Theory* (1997) Bart Moore-Gilbert contends that Spivak's reading of Bhubaneswari Bhaduri's unexplained suicide is a 'wishful use of history' (Moore-Gilbert 1997: 105). Like Varadharajan, Gilbert defines Spivak's use of deconstruction as 'a kind of "negative science"' (Moore-Gilbert 1997: 83), which cautions against incorporating the Other by assimilation into dominant systems of representation (Moore-Gilbert 1997: 102). Gilbert goes on to emphasise how subaltern silence paradoxically operates as a rhetorical strategy in Spivak's essay, for 'if Spivak's account of subaltern silence were true, then there would be nothing but the non-subaltern (particularly the West and the native elite) left to speak or write about' (Moore-Gilbert 1997: 104).

The attempt to theorise and rearticulate the unrepresented histories of subaltern women is further developed by Sandya Shetty and Elizabeth Jane Bellamy in their essay 'Postcolonialism's Archive Fever' (2000), which is perhaps the most rigorous reading of Spivak's essay to date. In their essay, Shetty and Bellamy focus on the importance of Spivak's deconstructive reading of the classic Hindu and Vedic scripts of antiquity on *sati* and widow-sacrifice. By doing so, they argue that Spivak measures the silences of the subaltern woman by re-articulating the originary archive of *sati* which is covered over in the subsequent palimpsest of misinterpretations and mistranslations authorised by the British colonial administration.

Most recently, at a symposium held at Columbia University in February 2002 on the ethico-political implications of the US war against Afghanistan since the bombing of the World Trade Centre in 2001, Spivak presented a paper on 'Terror'. In this paper, Spivak suggested that terror is the name given to the flip side of social movements against the legitimised terror of the State, and as such it is perhaps no more than an antonym for war. What is more, Spivak described how the global media is instrumental in constructing the non-relationship between the west ('us') and the 'Muslim world' ('them'). To counter the global media's destruction of an ethical relation to the Other, Spivak tried to rethink this geopolitical non-relationship based on the fear and terror of the Other through a deconstructive discourse of ethics and responsibility.

This analysis of the US war against Afghanistan could be seen to challenge Bart Moore-Gilbert's complaint that Spivak's thought is hampered by a reliance on Derrida's rethinking of ethics because it places the 'would-be non-subaltern ally of the subaltern' in an impossible double bind, where s/he cannot respond to the Otherness/alterity of the subaltern without silencing her (Moore-Gilbert 1997: 102). Instead, this recent paper points towards the possible advantages of Spivak's rethinking of ethics, politics and culture in the contemporary postcolonial world.

As one of the leading contemporary intellectuals of the late twentieth and early twenty-first centuries, Gayatri Spivak has persistently challenged the conventions and boundaries of western critical inquiry. With a polymath's command of Marxist political economics, feminism and postcolonial criticism, as well as European literature, philosophy and critical theory, Spivak has questioned the division between the act of reading literary and cultural texts and the economic text of imperialism and global capitalism. By invoking the historical exploitation and oppression of the disempowered, Spivak constantly reminds us that any act of reading has important social and political consequences.

FURTHER READING

This study has looked at some of the most important books, essays and interviews by Gayatri Spivak from the start of her career to the present. The following chapter provides a series of suggestions for further reading. Starting with an annotated list of Spivak's books, the chapter proceeds to list Spivak's numerous article publications (in journals and books), before providing a more detailed assessment of criticism and interpretation published about Spivak's thought. The separate works cited list at the end includes details of all the material referred to in this book. Please note that for the sake of clarity, all the essays and books by Spivak used as sources for quotations in the book are listed in this section only.

One of the best places to begin reading Spivak is *The Post-Colonial Critic*, a collection of interviews edited by Sarah Harasym. *The Spivak Reader* also contains a helpful introduction and textual commentaries on each of the essays included in the collection. For general background reading in postcolonial theory, the following books are recommended: Bill Ashcroft, Alan Lawson and Helen Tiffin's *The Empire Writes Back* (1989), Leela Gandhi's *Postcolonial Theory* (1998) and John McLeod's *Beginning Postcolonialism* (2000). For more detailed discussions of Spivak's thought in relation to postcolonial studies, Bart Moore-Gilbert's *Postcolonial Theory* (1997), Robert Young's *White Mythologies* (1990) and *Postcolonialism: An Historical Introduction* (2001) are suggested.

WORKS BY SPIVAK

BOOKS

Spivak, G.C. (1974) *Myself Must I Remake: The Life and Poetry of W. B. Yeats*, New York: Thomas Y. Crowell Co.

Based on Spivak's doctoral thesis, and published on 'a sixties impulse', this study (now out of print) examines the poetical works of the Irish poet W.B. Yeats.

—— (1976) *Of Grammatology* (translation with critical introduction of Jacques Derrida, *De la grammatologie*), Baltimore: Johns Hopkins.

This book launched Spivak's reputation as a theorist of deconstruction. The groundbreaking translation is accompanied by a comprehensive preface that covers most of the key concepts and intellectual influences in Derrida's early thought.

—— (1987) *In Other Worlds: Essays in Cultural Politics*, New York: Methuen.

Spivak's most well known and widely distributed book. Now in its fifth reprinting, this book contains some of Spivak's most important and influential essays on feminism, Marxism, deconstruction, the subaltern and the literary text. A key text.

—— (1988) *Selected Subaltern Studies*, edited with Ranajit Guha, New York: Oxford.

An edited selection of some of the essays published in the first five volumes of the Subaltern Studies series. 'Deconstructing Historiography', Spivak's critique of the Subaltern Studies collective, was published as the introduction to this text.

—— (1993) *Outside in the Teaching Machine*, New York: Routledge.

This book includes essays that revise some of Spivak's earlier positions in the 1980s on French feminism, the relationship between Marxism and deconstruction, and Michel Foucault. The book also includes essays on Salman Rushdie, Hanif Kureishi, Mahasweta Devi, and Cultural Studies. A key text.

—— (1995) *Imaginary Maps*, (translation with critical introduction of three stories by Mahasweta Devi), New York: Routledge.

A collection of three stories by Mahasweta Devi, translated by Spivak. The book also includes a translator's preface and afterword by

Spivak, in which Spivak develops an ethics of reading the subaltern and locates Devi's writing in relation to aboriginal tribal communities in Bengal.

—— (1997) *Old Women*, (translation with critical introduction of two stories by Mahasweta Devi), Calcutta: Seagull.

Another collection of stories by Mahasweta Devi, translated by Gayatri Spivak.

—— (1997) *The Breast Stories*, (translation with critical introduction of three stories by Mahasweta Devi), Calcutta: Seagull.

Another collection of stories by Mahasweta Devi, translated by Gayatri Spivak. This essay contains a revised version of 'A Literary Representation of the Subaltern', Spivak's reading of Mahasweta Devi's 'Breast Giver'.

—— (1999) *A Critique of Postcolonial Reason: Towards a History of the Vanishing Present*, Cambridge: Harvard University Press; Calcutta: Seagull Press.

Spivak's magnum opus. This challenging text revises many of Spivak's earlier writings on literature and the subaltern, but also includes stunning new readings of German philosophy, the colonial archives, Cultural Studies and globalisation. A key text.

ARTICLES

Spivak has published a vast number of articles and continues to write. It would not be practical to annotate every entry in this list, but you will notice that certain articles have been reprinted in various readers or essay collections. In this book, many of these articles are cited from essay collections such as *In Other Worlds*, *The Post-Colonial Critic* and *A Critique of Postcolonial Reason*, or readers such as *The Spivak Reader*, rather than the original articles (see Works cited). Indeed, it might be easier to approach these essays through the collections and readers in which they appear, as the editors will usually have offered some form of discussion or introductory note.

Spivak, G.C. (1965) 'Shakespeare in Yeats's *Last Poems*', *Shakespeare Memorial Volume*, Calcutta Presidency College, pp.243–84.

—— (1968) '"Principles of the Mind": Continuity in Yeats's Poetry', *Modern Language Notes*, December, pp.282–99.

—— (1970) 'Versions of a Colossus', *Journal of South Asian Literature* (VI) pp.31–7.

—— (1971) 'Allégorie et histoire de la poésie: hypothèse de travail', *Poètique* (VIII) pp.427–44.

—— (1972) 'A Stylistic Contrast Between Yeats and Mallarmé', *Language and Style* (v.II) Spring, pp.100–7.

—— (1972) 'Thoughts on the Principle of Allegory', *Genre*, December, pp.327–52.

—— (1973) 'Indo-Anglian Curiosities', *Novel* (VII.i) Fall, pp.91–3.

—— (1973) 'The Liberal Arts: Liberating or Confining?' *The Grinnel Magazine*, November–December, pp.15–16.

—— (1974) 'Decadent Style', *Language and Style* (VII.iv) Fall, pp.227–34.

—— (1975) 'Some Theoretical Aspects of Yeats's Prose', *Journal of Modern Literature* (IV.iii) February, pp.667–91.

—— (1977) '*Glas*-Piece: A Compte-Rendu', *Diacritics* (VII.iii) Fall, pp.22–43.

—— (1977) 'The Letter as Cutting Edge', *Yale French Studies*, (LV/LVI) pp.208–26; reprinted in Shoshana Felman (ed.), *Literature and Psychoanalysis: Reading Otherwise*, New Haven: Yale University Press, 1982, pp.208–26; reprinted in Spivak 1987.

—— (1978) 'Anarchism Revisited: A New Philosophy', *Diacritics*, (VII.ii) Summer, pp.66–79 (with Michael Ryan).

—— (1978) 'Feminism and Critical Theory', *Women's Studies International Quarterly* (I) pp.241–6; reprinted in Spivak 1987.

—— (1979) 'Explanation and Culture: Marginalia', *Humanities in Society*, (II.iii) Summer, pp.201–21; reprinted in Sowon Kwon (ed.), *Out There: Marginalisation and Contemporary Cultures*, Cambridge: MIT Press, 1990, pp.377–93; reprinted in Spivak 1987.

—— (1979/80) 'Three Feminist Readings: McCuller, Drabble, Habermas', *Union Seminary Quarterly Review* (XXXV.i,ii) Fall/Winter, pp.15–34; reprinted in Spivak 1987.

—— (1979/80) Review Essay on Robert R. Magliola, *Phenomenology and Literature: An Introduction, Modern Fiction Studies* (XXV.iv) Winter, pp.758–60.

—— (1980) 'A Dialogue on the Production of Literary Journals, the Division of the Disciplines and Ideology Critique with Professors Gayatri Spivak, Bill Galston and Michael Ryan', *Analecta* (VI) pp.72–87.

—— (1980) 'Unmaking and Making in *To the Lighthouse*', *Women and Language in Literature and Society* (ed.), Sally McConnel-Ginet *et al.*, New York: Praeger Publishers, pp.310–27; reprinted in Spivak 1987.

—— (1980) 'Revolutions That As Yet Have No Model: Derrida's *Limited Inc.*', *Diacritics* (X.iv) Winter, pp.29–49; reprinted in Spivak 1996.

—— (1980) 'Finding Feminist Readings: Dante–Yeats', *Social Text* (III) Fall, pp.73–87; reprinted in Spivak 1987.

—— (1981) '"Draupadi" by Mahasweta Devi', *Critical Inquiry*, (VII.ii) Winter, pp.381–402; reprinted in Elizabeth Abel (ed.), *Writing and Difference*, Chicago: University of Chicago Press: 1982; reprinted in Dilip K. Basu and Richard Sisson (eds), *Social and Economic Development*, New Delhi: Sage, 1986, pp.215–40; reprinted in Spivak 1987.

—— (1981) 'French Feminism in an International Frame', *Yale French Studies*, (62) pp.154–84; reprinted in Camille Roman, Suzanne Juhasz and Cristanne Miller (eds), *The Women and Language Debate: A Sourcebook*, New Brunswick: Rutgers University Press, 1993, pp.101–4; reprinted in Sandra Kemp and Judith Squires (eds), *Oxford Readers: Feminisms*, Oxford: Oxford University Press, 1998, pp.51–4; reprinted in Spivak 1987.

—— (1981) 'Il faut s'y prendre en s'en prennant à elles', *Les Fins de l'homme*, Phillipe Lacoue-Labarthe and Jean Luc Nancy (eds), Paris: Galilée, pp.505–16.

—— (1981) 'Reading the World: Literary Studies in the 80s', *College English* (XLIII.vii) November, pp.671–9; reprinted in G. Douglas Atkins and Michael L. Johnson (eds), *Writing and Reading Differently: Deconstruction and the Teaching of Composition and Literature*, Lawrence, Kansas: University Press of Kansas, 1985; reprinted in Spivak 1987.

—— (1981) 'Sex and History in *The Prelude* (1805), Books Nine to Thirteen', *Texas Studies in Literature and Language* (XXII.iii) Fall, pp.324–60; reprinted in Christopher Norris and Richard Machin (eds), *Post-Structuralist Readings of English Poetry*, Cambridge: Cambridge University Press, 1987, pp.193–226; reprinted in Spivak 1987.

—— (1982) 'The Politics of Interpretations', *Critical Inquiry* (IX.i) September, pp.259–78; reprinted in W. J. T. Mitchell (ed.), *The Politics of Interpretation*, Chicago: University of Chicago Press, 1983; reprinted in Esther Fuchs (ed.), *Feminist Hermeneutics: A Multidisciplinary Approach* (forthcoming); reprinted in Spivak 1987.

—— (1983) 'Marx After Derrida', William E. Cain (ed.), *Philosophical Approaches to Literature: New Essays on Nineteenth and Twentieth Century Texts*, Lewisberg, Pennsylvania: Bucknell University Press, pp.227–46.

—— (1983) 'Review Essay on Beatrice Farnsworth, *On Aleksandra Kollontai*, *Minnesota Review* (n.s.20) Spring, pp.93–102.

—— (1983) 'Some Thoughts on Evaluation', Mark Axelrod *et al.* (eds), *CLAM Chowder*, Minneapolis: Comparative Literature Association of Minnesota, pp.60–74.

—— (1983) 'Displacement and the Discourse of Woman', Mark Krupnick (ed.), *Displacement: Derrida and After,* Bloomington: University of Indiana Press, pp.169–95; reprinted in Anthony Easthope and Kate McGowan (eds), *A Critical and Cultural Theory Reader*, Toronto: University of Toronto Press, 1992; reprinted in Nancy J. Holland (ed.), *Feminist Interpretations of Jacques Derrida*, College Park: Pennsylvania State University Press, 1997, pp.43–71.

—— (1984) 'A Response to John O'Neill', Gary Shapiro and Alan Sica (eds), *Hermeneutics: Questions and Prospects*, Amherst: University of Massachusetts Press, pp.19–36.

—— (1984) 'Descriptions and Its Vicissitudes', review article on Marc Eli Blanchard, *Description, Sign, Self, Desire: Critical Theory in the Wake of Semiotics, Semiotica* (XLIX, iii/iv) pp.347–60.

—— (1984) 'Love Me, Love My Ombre, Elle', *Diacritics* (XIV.iv) Winter, pp.19–36.

—— (1984/85) 'Criticism , Feminism and the Institution', (interview with Elizabeth Grosz) *Thesis Eleven* (10/11) pp.175–87; reprinted in Spivak 1990.

—— (1985) 'Can the Subaltern Speak? Speculations on Widow-Sacrifice', *Wedge* (7/8) Winter/Spring, pp.120–30.

—— (1985) 'Feminism and Critical Theory', Paula Treichler *et al.* (ed.), *For Alma Mater: Theory and Practice in Feminist Scholarship*, Urbana: University of Illinois Press, pp.119–42; reprinted in Robert Con Davis and Ronald Schleifer (eds), *Contemporary Literary Criticism: Literary and Cultural Studies*, New York: Longman, 1994, pp.519–34; excerpt reprinted in David Lodge and Nigel Wood (eds), *Modern Criticism and Theory: a Reader*, Harlow: Longman, 1999; reprinted in Spivak 1987 and Spivak 1996.

—— (1985) 'Scattered Speculations on the Question of Value', *Diacritics* (XV.iv) Winter, pp.73–93; reprinted in Spivak 1987 and Spivak 1996.

—— (1985) 'Strategies of Vigilance' (Interview), Block 10, pp.20–33; reprinted in Spivak 1990.

—— (1985) 'Subaltern Studies: Deconstructing Historiography', Ranajit Guha (ed.), *Subaltern Studies IV: Writings on South Asian History and Society*, New Delhi: Oxford University Press, pp.330–63; reprinted in Jessica Munns and Gita Rajan (eds), *Cultural Studies: An Anglo American Reader*, Essex: Longman, forthcoming; reprinted in *Selected Subaltern Studies*, Guha and Spivak (eds) Oxford: Oxford University Press, 1988; and in Spivak 1987.

—— (1985) 'The Rani of Sirmur: An Essay in Reading the Archives', *History and Theory* (XXIV, 3) 1985, pp.247–72; reprinted in Francis Barker *et al.* (eds), *Europe and Its Others*, Colchester: University of Essex Press, 1985, pp.128–51.

—— (1985) 'Three Women's Texts and a Critique of Imperialism', *Critical Inquiry* (XII.i) Autumn, pp.243–61; reprinted in Catherine Belsey and Jane Moore (eds), *The Feminist Reader: Essays in Gender and the Politics of Literary Criticism*, London: Blackwell, 1989; in Norwegian translation from the University of Oslo Press; in Diane Price Herndl and Robyn Warhol (eds), *Feminisms: an Anthology of Literary Theory and Criticism*, New Brunswick: Rutgers University Press, 2nd edition, 1997, pp.896–912; revised extract in Fred Botting (ed.), *Frankenstein*, London: Macmillan New Casebooks, 1995, pp.235–60; reprinted in Bill Ashcroft *et al.* (eds), *The Post Colonial Studies Reader*, London:

Routledge, 1995, pp.262–70.; reprinted in Bart Moore-Gilbert (ed.), *Post Colonial Theory*, London: Longman, 1996; reprinted in Chinese translation in *Chung-Wai Literary Monthly*, Taiwan (24.5) October 1995, pp.6–21; extract reprinted in Peter Brooker and Peter Widdowson (eds), *A Practical Reader in Contemporary Literary Theory*, Englewood: Prentice Hall, 1996; excerpt reprinted as 'Frankenstein and a Critique of Imperialism', in J. Paul Hunter (ed.), *Frankenstein*, New York: Norton Critical Edition, 1996, pp.262–70; reprinted in Judith Raiskin (ed.) Jean Rhys, *Wide Sargasso Sea*, New York: Norton Critical Edition, 1999, pp.240–7; reprinted in Diana Brydon (ed.), *Postcolonialism: Critical Concepts*, New York: Routledge, 2000.

—— (1986) 'Imperialism and Sexual Difference', *Oxford Literary Review* (VII. i–ii) pp.225–40; reprinted in Clayton Koelb and Virgil Lokke (eds), *The Current in Criticism: Essays in the Present and Future of Literary Theory*, West Lafayette: Purdue University Press, 1988, pp.319–37; reprinted in Robert Con Davis and Ronald Schleifer (eds), *Contemporary Literary Criticism: Literary and Cultural Studies*, New York: Longman, 1989.

—— (1986) 'Interview with Patrice McDermott', *Art Papers*, (X.i) January–February, pp.50–2.

—— (1986) 'Literature, Theory and Commitment: III', in Kenneth Harrow, *et al.* (eds), *Crisscrossing Boundaries in African Literatures*, Washington DC: African Literature Association, pp.71–5.

—— (1987) 'Speculations on Reading Marx: After Reading Derrida', Derek Attridge *et al.* (eds), *Post-Structuralism and the Question of History*, Cambridge: Cambridge University Press, pp.30–62.

—— (1988) 'A Literary Representation of the Subaltern', Ranajit Guha (ed.), *Subaltern Studies*, New Delhi: Oxford University Press, vol. V; translation of embedded fiction ('Breast-giver', by Mahasweta Devi) reprinted in Susan Thames and Marin Gazzaniga (eds), *The Breast: an Anthology*, New York: Global City Press, 1995, pp.86–111; reprinted in Spivak 1987.

—— (1988) 'A Response to "The Difference Within: Feminism and Critical Theory"', in Elizabeth Meece and Alice Parker (eds), *The Difference Within: Feminism and Critical Theory*, Amsterdam/Philadelphia: John Benjamins, pp.208–20.

—— (1988) 'Can the Subaltern Speak?' in *Marxism and the Interpretation of Culture*, Cary Nelson and Larry Grossberg (eds), Urbana: University of Illinois Press, pp.271–313; reprinted in Patrick Williams and Laura Chrisman (eds), *Colonial Discourse and Post-Colonial Theory: A Reader*, New York: Harvester/Wheatsheaf, 1994, pp.66–111; reprinted in Chinese translation, *Chung-Wai Literary Monthly* (XXIV.vi) 1995, pp.94–123; forthcoming in Hebrew translation.

—— (1988) 'Practical Politics of the Open End: an Interview with Gayatri Chakravorty Spivak', by Sarah Harasym, *Canadian Journal of Political and Social Theory* (XII.i–ii) pp.51–69; reprinted in Spivak 1990.

—— (1988) 'The *Intervention* Interview', *Southern Humanities Review* (XXII.iv) Fall, pp.323–42; reprinted in Spivak 1990.

—— (1989) 'Colloquium on Narrative' (Interview), *Typereader* (3) December, pp.21–38.

—— (1989) 'Feminism and Deconstruction Again', in Teresa Brennan (ed.), *Between Feminism and Psychoanalysis*, London: Methuen, pp.206–23; reprinted in *Outside in the Teaching Machine*.

—— (1989) 'In A Word. *Interview*' (with Ellen Rooney), *Differences*, (I.ii) Summer, pp.124–56; reprinted in *the essential difference*, Bloomington: Indiana University Press, 1994, pp.151–85; reprinted in revised form in Terry Lovell (ed.), *Feminist Cultural Studies*, Brookfield, Vermont: E. Elgar (2) 1995, pp.162–88; reprinted in revised version with Linda Nicholson (ed.), *Feminist Theory and the Second Wave*, New York: Routledge, 1996, pp.356–78; reprinted in *Outside in the Teaching Machine*.

—— (1989) 'In Praise of *Sammy and Rosie Get Laid*', *Critical Quarterly* (XXXI.ii) Summer, pp.80–8; reprinted in *Outside in the Teaching Machine*.

—— (1989) 'Naming Gayatri Spivak' (Interview), *Stanford Humanities Review* (I.i) Spring, pp.84–97.

—— (1989) 'Negotiating the Structures of Violence: A Conversation with Gayatri Chakravorty Spivak' (Interview), *Polygraph* (II–III) Spring, pp.218–29; reprinted in Spivak 1990.

—— (1989) 'Poststructuralism, Marginality, Postcoloniality and Value', in Peter Collier and Helga Geyer-Ryan (eds), *Literary Theory Today*, Cambridge: Polity Press, 1990; reprinted in *Sociocriticism* (X) pp.43–81; reprinted in Padmini Mongia (ed.), *Contemporary Postcolonial Theory: A Reader*, New York: Arnold Press, 1996, pp.198–364; reprinted in *Outside in the Teaching Machine*.

—— (1989) 'Questions of Multiculturalism', in Angela Ingram (ed.), *Women's Writing in Exile*, Chapel Hill: University of North Carolina, pp.412–20; reprinted in Spivak 1990.

—— (1989) 'Reading the *Satanic Verses*', *Public Culture* (II.i) Fall, pp.79–99; revised and expanded version in *Third Text* (11) 1990, pp.41–69; reprinted in Maurice Biriotti and Nicola Miller (eds), *What is an Author?*, Manchester: Manchester University Press, 1993; shortened version printed in Nigel Wheale (ed.), *The Postmodern Arts?*, London: Routledge, 1994, pp.221–43; reprinted in *Outside in the Teaching Machine*.

—— (1989) 'The New Historicism: Political Commitment and the Postmodern Critic', in H. Aram Veeser (ed.), *The New Historicism*, New York: Routledge, pp.277–92; reprinted in Spivak 1990.

—— (1989) 'The Political Economy of Women as Seen by a Literary Critic', in Elizabeth Weed (ed.), *Coming to Terms: Feminism, Theory, Politics*, London: Routledge, pp.218–29.

—— (1989) 'Who Claims Alterity?', in Barbara Kruger and Phil Mariani (eds), *Remaking History*, Dia Art Foundation Discussions in Contemporary Culture No. 4, Seattle: Bay Press, pp.269–92; reprinted in Heliosa Buarque de Hollanda (ed.), *Feminism as Cultural Critique*, Rio de Janeiro: CIEC, forthcoming, pp.187–205; reprinted in Charles Harrison *et al.* (eds), *Art in Theory*, Oxford: Blackwell, 1997, pp.1119–24.

—— (1989) 'Who Needs the Great Works? A Debate on the Canon, Core Curricula and Culture', *Harpers* (279.1672) September, pp.43–52.

—— (1989) Lukas Barr, 'An Interview with Gayatri Chakravorty Spivak', *Blast Unlimited* (I) Summer, pp.6–8.

—— (1989/90) 'Woman In Difference: Mahasweta Devi's "Douloti the Bountiful"', *Cultural Critique* (XIV) Winter, pp.105–28; reprinted in Andrew Parker (ed.), *Nationalisms and Sexuality*, New York: Routledge, 1992, pp.96–117; reprinted in German translation in *Polylog* (forthcoming); reprinted in *Outside in the Teaching Machine*.

—— (1990) 'An Interview with Gayatri Spivak', *Women and Performance* (v.i) pp.80–92.

—— (1990) 'Constitutions and Culture Studies', *Yale Journal of Law and Humanities* (II.i) Winter, pp.133–47; reprinted in Jerry D. Leonard (ed.), *Legal Studies as Cultural Studies: A Reader in (Post)Modern Critical Theory*, Albany: SUNY Press, 1995, pp.155–74.

—— (1990) 'Gayatri Spivak on the Politics of the Subaltern', *Socialist Review* (XX.iii) July–September, pp.85–97.

—— (1990) 'Inscriptions: of Truth to Size', Catalogue essay for *Inscriptions* by Jamelie Hassan, Regina: Dunlop Art Gallery, pp.9–34; reprinted in *Outside in the Teaching Machine*.

—— (1990) 'Rhetoric and Cultural Explanation: A Discussion', with Phillip Sipiora and Janet Atwill, *Journal of Advance Composition* (X.ii) Fall, pp.293–304.

—— (1990) 'The Making of Americans, the Teaching of English, and the Future of Culture Studies', *New Literary History* (XXI.iv) Autumn, pp.781–98; reprinted in *Outside in the Teaching Machine*.

—— (1990) 'Versions of the Margin: J.M. Coetzee's *Foe* Reading of Defoe's *Crusoe/Roxana*', Jonathan Arac and Barbara Johnson (eds), *Consequences of Theory: Selected Papers of the English Institute, 1987–88*, Baltimore: Johns Hopkins University Press, pp.154–80; reprinted in 'Theory in the Margin: Coetzee's *Foe* Reading of Defoe's *Crusoe/Roxana*', *English in Africa* (XVII.ii) October 1990, pp.1–23.

—— (1991) 'Identity and Alterity: An Interview', *Arena* (97) pp.65–76.

—— (1991) 'Neocolonialism and the Secret Agent of Knowledge: an Interview with Gayatri Chakravorty Spivak', *Oxford Literary Review* (XII.i–ii) pp.220–51.

——— (1991) 'Not Virgin Enough to Say That [S]he Occupies the Place of the Other', *Cardozo Law Review* (XIII.iv) December, pp.1343–8; reprinted in *Outside in the Teaching Machine*.

——— (1991) 'Once Again a Leap into the Postcolonial Banal', *Differences* (III.iii) Fall, pp.139–70 (with cultural commentary by Joan Scott); revised version reprinted as 'How to Teach a "Culturally Different" Book', in Peter Hulme (ed.), *Colonial Discourse/ Post-Colonial Theory*, Manchester: Manchester University Press, 1994, pp.126–50.

——— (1991) 'Reflections of Cultural Studies in the Post-Colonial Conjuncture', *Critical Studies* (III.i–ii) Spring, pp.63–78.

——— (1991) 'Time and Timing: Law and History', in John Bender and David Wellbery (eds), *Chronotypes: The Construction of Time*, Stanford: Stanford University Press, pp.99–117.

——— (1992) 'Acting Bits/Identity Talk', *Critical Inquiry* (XVIII.iv) Summer, pp.770–803; reprinted in Henry Louis Gates Jr. and Anthony Appiah (eds), *Identities*, Chicago: University of Chicago Press, 1995, pp.147–80; reprinted in revised form in Denis Crowe (ed.), *Geography and Identity: Living and Exploring Geopolitics of Identity*, Washington: Maisonneuve, 1996, pp.41–72; reprinted in Robert Lumsden and Rajeev Patke (eds), *Critical Studies*, Amsterdam/Atlanta: Rodopi, 1996, pp.295–338.

——— (1992) 'Asked to Talk About Myself . . .', *Third Text* (XIX) Summer, pp.9–18.

——— (1992) 'French Feminism Revisited: Ethics and Politics', in Joan Scott and Judith Butler (eds), *Feminists Theorise the Political*, New York: Routledge, pp.54–85; reprinted in revised form as 'Cixous Without Borders', in Mireille Calle (ed.), *On the Feminine*, translated by Catherine McGann, Atlantic Highlands Humanities Press, 1996, pp.46–56; reprinted in *Outside in the Teaching Machine*.

——— (1992) 'More on Power/Knowledge', in Thomas E. Wartenburg (ed.), *Rethinking Power*, Albany: SUNY Press, pp.149–73; reprinted in *Outside in the Teaching Machine*.

——— (1992) 'Teaching for the Times', *MMLA* (XXV.i) pp.3–22; reprinted with extensive revisions in Jan Nederveen Pieterse (ed.), *The Decolonization of Imagination*, London: Zed Books, 1995, pp.177–202;

extract reprinted in Pavel Büchler and Nikos Papasterigiadis (eds), *Random Access 2: Ambient Fears*, London: Rivers Oram Press, 1996, pp.189–204; reprinted in Anne McClintock *et al.* (eds), *Dangerous Liaisons: Gender, Nation and the Post-Colonial Perspectives*, Minneapolis: University of Minnesota Press, 1997, pp.468–90.

—— (1992) 'The Burden of English', in Rajeswari Sunder Rajan (ed.), *The Lie of the Land: English Literary Studies in India*, Delhi: Oxford University Press, pp.275–99; reprinted in revised version in Carol Breckenridge and Peter van der Veer (eds), *Orientalism and the Postcolonial Predicament: Perspectives on South Asia*, Philadelphia: University of Pennsylvania Press, 1993, pp.134–57.

—— (1992) 'The Politics of Translation', in Michèle Barret and Anne Philips (eds), *Destabilising Theory: Contemporary Feminist Debates*, Cambridge: Polity Press, pp.177–200; revised version reprinted in Jessica Munns *et al.*, *Cultural Studies: A British-American Reader*, London: Longmans, forthcoming; German translation reprinted in Anselm Haverkampf (ed.), *Die Sprache des Anderen*, Frankfurt: Fischer, 1995, pp.65–93; included in Spanish translation in the volume published by Programa Universitario de Estudios de Genero, 1997; reprinted in Lawrence Venuti (ed.), *The Translation Studies Reader*, New York: Routledge, 2000; reprinted in *Outside in the Teaching Machine*.

—— (1992) Entry on Bookwork, *Jamelie/Jamila Project* by J. Hassan and J. Ismail, North Vancouver: Presentation House Gallery.

—— (1992) 'Extreme Eurocentrism', *Lusitania*, (I.iv): 55–60.

—— (1992) *Thinking Academic Freedom in Gendered Post-Coloniality*, Cape Town: University of Capetown Press; revised version reprinted in *Pretexts* (V.i–ii) 1995, pp.117–56.

—— (1993) 'An Interview with Gayatri Chakravorty Spivak', Sara Danius and Stefan Jonsson, *boundary 2* (XX.ii) Summer, pp.24–50.

—— (1993) 'Echo', *New Literary History* (XXIV.i) Winter, pp.17–43; reprinted in E. Ann Kaplan (ed.), *Psychoanalysis and Cultural Studies*, Cheltenham: Edward Elgar, 1995; partially reprinted in German translation in *Die Philosophin,* (13) May 1996, pp.68–96.

—— (1993) 'Excelsior Hotel Coffee Shop', *Assemblage*, (20) April, pp.74–5.

—— (1993) 'Foundations and Cultural Studies', in Hugh J. Silverman (ed.), *Questioning Foundations: Truth/Subjectivity/Culture*, New York: Routledge, pp.153–75.

—— (1993) 'Questions of Multiculturalism', An Interview with Gayatri Chakravorty Spivak and Sneja Gunew in Simon During (ed.), *The Cultural Studies Reader*, New York: Routledge, pp.193–202.

—— (1993) 'Race before Racism and the Disappearance of the American: Jack D. Forbes', *Black Africans and Americans: Color, Race and Caste in the Evolution of Red-Black Peoples*', *Plantation Society* (III.ii) Summer, pp.73–91; reprinted in *boundary 2* (XXV.ii Edward Said issue) Summer 1998, pp.35–53.

—— (1993) 'Situations of Value: Feminism and Cultural Work in a Postcolonial Neocolonial Conjuncture' (Interview), *Australian Feminist Studies* (XVII) Autumn, pp.141–61.

—— (1994) '"What Is It For?": Functions of the Postcolonial Critic', *Nineteenth Century Contexts* (XVIII) pp.71–81.

—— (1994) 'Återbesök i den globalal byn', in Oscar Hemer (ed.), *Kulturen i den globala* byn, Lund: Ægis Förlag, pp.165–88.

—— (1994) 'Bonding in Difference', in Alfred Arteaga (ed.), *An Other Tongue*, Durham: Duke University Press, pp.273–85; reprinted in Spivak 1996.

—— (1994) 'In the New World Order: A Speech', in Antonio Callari *et al.*, *Marxism in the Postmodern Age: Confronting the New World Order*, New York: Guilford Press, pp.89–97.

—— (1994) 'Introduction', in Harriet Fraad *et al.* (eds), *Bringing It All Back Home: Class Gender and Power in the Modern Household*, London: Pluto Press, pp.ix–xvi.

—— (1994) 'Psychoanalysis in Left Field; and Field-Working: Examples to Fit the Title', in Michael Münchow and Sonu Shamdasani (eds), *Speculations After Freud: Psychoanalysis, Philosophy and Culture*, London: Routledge, pp.41–75; reprinted as 'Examples to Fit the Title', in *American Imago* (LI.ii) Summer 1994, pp.161–96.

—— (1994) 'Response to Jean-Luc Nancy', in Juliet Flower MacCannell and Laura Zakarin (eds), *Thinking Bodies*, Stanford: Stanford University Press, pp.32–51.

—— (1994) 'Responsibility', *boundary 2* (XXI.iii) Fall, pp.19–64; reprinted in Spanish translation in *Nueva Sociedad*, Caracas, Venezuela, pp.49–119; reprinted in Silvestra Mariniello and Paul A. Bové (eds), *Gendered Agents: Women and Institutional Knowledge*, Durham and London: Duke University Press, 1998, pp.19–66.

—— (1994) 'Tribal Woes', *Economic Times*, April 13: 10, 26; reprinted from *Imaginary Maps*.

—— (1995) '"Woman" as Theatre: Beijing 1995', *Radical Philosophy* (LXX) November, pp.2–4; reprinted in German translation in *epd-Endwicklungspolitik-Materialien* (II) 1996, pp.56–9.

—— (1995) 'A Dialogue on Democracy', with David Plotke, *Socialist Review* (XCIV.iii) pp.1–22; reprinted in David Trend (ed.), *Radical Democracy: Identity, Citizenship and the State*, New York: Routledge, 1995, pp.209–22.

—— (1995) 'At the *Planchette* of Deconstruction Is/In America', in Anselm Haverkamf (ed.), *Deconstruction is/in America: A New Sense of the Political*, New York: New York University Press, pp.237–49.

—— (1995) 'Empowering Women?' *Environment* (XXXVII.i) January/February, pp.2–3.

—— (1995) 'Ghostwriting', *Diacritics* (XXV.ii) Summer, pp.65–84.

—— (1995) 'Love, Cruelty and Cultural Talks in the Hot Peace', *Parallax 1*, November, pp.1–31; extract reprinted in Pheng Cheah and Bruce Robbins (eds), *Cosmopoloitics: Thinking and Feeling Beyond the Nation*, Minneapolis: University of Minnesota Press, 1998, pp.329–48.

—— (1995) 'Running Interference', interview with Julie Stephens, *Australian Women's Book Review* (VII.ii) June: 19–22 and (VII.ii.iv) November 1995, pp.26–8; reprinted in longer form as 'Cultural Dominance at its Most Benevolent', interview with Julie Stephens, *Arena Journal*, New Series (6) 1996, pp.35–50.

—— (1995) 'Supplementing Marxism', in Steven Cullenberg and Bernd Magnus (eds), *Whither Marxism?*, New York: Routledge, pp.109–19.

—— (1996) 'Diasporas Old and New: Women in a Transnational World', *Textual Practice* (X.ii) pp.245–69; reprinted in Amitava Kumar (ed.), *Class Issues: Pedagogy, Cultural Studies and the Public Sphere*, New York: New York Univeristy Press, 1997, pp.87–116; reprinted in Peter Trifonis (ed.), Routledge, forthcoming; reprinted in Portuguese translation in Vera Queiroz (ed.), *Critica Literária Feminista Anglo-Americana*, Brazil: CNPq, forthcoming.

—— (1996) 'Further Notes on "Imperialism Today"', *Against the Current* (XI.iii) July–August, pp.20–1.

—— (1996) 'Lives', in H. Aram Veeser (ed.), *Confessions of the Critics*, New York: Routledge, pp.205–20.

—— (1996) 'Setting to Work (Transnational Cultural Studies)', in Peter Osborne (ed.), *A Critical Sense: Interviews with Intellectuals*, London: Routledge, pp.163–77.

—— (1996) 'Transnationality and the Multiculturalist Ideology', in Deepika Bahri and Mary Vasudeva (eds), *Between the Lines: South Asians and Postcoloniality*, Philadelphia: Temple University Press, pp.64–88.

—— (1997) 'Abinirman-Anubad', *Paschimbanga Bangla Akademi Patrika* (X) November, pp.17–33.

—— (1997) 'At Home With Others', catalogue essay for exhibition on 'Dislocations', Rovaniemi Art Museum, Rovaniemi, Finland.

—— (1997) 'City, Country, Agency', in Vikramaditya Prakash (ed.), *Theatres of Decolonisation: (Architectural Agency [Urbanism])*, Seattle: University of Washington Press, pp.760–9.

—— (1997) 'Of Poetics and Politics', *Politics–Poetics: Documenta X*, Ostfildern-Ruit: Cantz, pp.760–9.

—— (1997) 'Scattered Speculations on the Question of Linguisti-culture', in Takayuki Yokota-Murakami (ed.), *Linguisticulture: Where Do We Go From Here?*, Osaka: Univeristy of Osaka Press.

—— (1997/98) 'Attention: Postcolonialism!', *Journal of Caribbean Studies* (XII.ii–iii) Fall/Spring, pp.159–70; in German translation in Peter Weibel and Slavoj Zizek (eds), *Inklusion Exklusion: Probleme des Postkolonialismus und der Globalen Migration*, Vienna: Passagen, 1997, pp.117–30.

—— (1998) 'Feminist Literary Criticism', in Edward Craig (ed.), *Routledge Encyclopedia of Philosophy* (vol. 3), New York: Routledge, pp.611–4.

—— (1998) 'Foucault and Najibullah', in Kathy Komar and Ross Shidler (eds), *Lyrical Symbols and Narrative Transformations: Essays in Honour of Ralph Freedman*, Columbia: Camden House, pp.218–35.

—— (1998) 'Lost Our Language – Underneath the Linguistic Map', in Rainer Ganahl (ed.), *Imported: A Reading Seminar*, New York: Semiotext[e], pp.182–93.

—— (1998) 'The Setting to Work of Deconstruction', in Michael Kelly (ed.), *Encyclopedia of Aesthetics Volume Two*, Oxford: Oxford University Press, 4 vols, pp.7–11; reprinted in *A Critique of Postcolonial Reason*.

—— (1999) 'American Gender Studies Today' (with Camille Paglia, Donna Landry and Jane Gallop), *Women: A Cultural Review* (X.ii) pp.213–9.

—— (1999) 'Circumfessions: My Story as the (M)other's Story', in Alfred Hornung, Ernstpeter Ruhe (eds), *Postcolonialisme and Autobiographie: Michelle Cliff, David Dabydeen, Opal Palmer Adisa*, Amsterdam: Editions Rodopi.

—— (1999) 'From Primrose Hill Flat to US Classroom, What's Left of Theory?', in Judith Butler *et al.* (eds), *What's Left of Theory?: New Work on the Politics of Literary Theory*, Papers of the English Institute, New York and London: Routledge, pp.1–39.

—— (1999) 'Imperatives to Re-Imagine the Planet/Imperative zur Neuerfindung des Planeten', Willi Goetschel, (ed.), Vienna: Passagen; reprinted in Len Gunter and Cornelius Heesters, *Social Insecurities*, Toronto: Anansi, 1999.

—— (1999) 'Moving Devi', in Vidya Dehejia (ed.), *Devi: The Great Goddess*, Washington: Smithsonian Institute, pp.181–200; expanded version forthcoming in *Cultural Critique*.

—— (1999) 'Thinking Cultural Questions in "Pure" Literary Terms', in Paul Gilroy *et al.* (eds), *Without Guarantees: Essays in Honor of Stuart Hall*, London: Verso, pp.335–57.

—— (1999) 'Translation as Culture', in Isabel Carrera Suarez, Aurora Garcia Fernandez and M.S. Suarez Lafuente, (eds), *Translating Cultures*, Oviedo: KRK Ediciones; Hebden Bridge, UK: Dangaroo Press, 1999, pp.17–30; reprinted in *Parallax: A Journal of Metadiscursive Theory and Cultural Practices,* January–March 2000 (14) pp.13–34.

—— (2000) 'Claiming Transformations', in Sara Ahmed *et al.* (eds), *Transformation: Thinking Through Feminism*, London: Routledge.

—— (2000) 'Arguments for a Deconstructive Cultural Studies', in Nicholas Royle (ed.), *Deconstructions*, Oxford: Blackwell, pp.14–43.

—— (2000) 'The New Subaltern: A Silent Interview', in Vinayak Chaturvedi (ed.), *Mapping Subaltern Studies and The Postcolonial*, London: Verso, pp.324–41.

—— (2000) 'A Moral Dilemma' in Howard Marchitello (ed.), *What Happens to History: The Renewal of Ethics in Contemporary Thought*, London and New York: Routledge.

WORKS ON SPIVAK

Ashcroft, Bill, Lawson, Alan and Tiffin, Helen (1989) *The Empire Writes Back*, London: Routledge.

This book is one of the first introductory guides to postcolonial literary criticism in English. It contains a short discussion of Spivak's contribution to postcolonial and feminist reading practices. A useful introduction to postcolonial criticism and theory.

Chow, R. (1993) 'Ethics after Idealism', *Diacritics* 23 (1) pp.3–22.

Includes an insightful chapter comparing Spivak's deconstructive re-reading of Marx to Slavoj Zizek's re-thinking of ideology criticism through Lacanian psychoanalysis.

Gandhi, L. (1998) *Postcolonial Theory: A Critical Introduction*, New York and Chichester: Columbia University Press.

This introduction to postcolonial theory contains a lucid chapter on feminism that places Spivak's work in relation to Third World feminist criticism.

Harasym, Sarah (ed.) (1990) *The Post-Colonial Critic: Interviews, Strategies, Dialogues*, New York and London: Routledge.

A collection of interviews with Spivak, conducted during the 1980s by philosophers, literary critics, feminist scholars and postcolonial thinkers, this book covers a range of topics and contains insightful discussions of Spivak's key ideas. The book also highlights Spivak's contribution to the emerging field of postcolonial studies. A key text.

Landry, Donna and Maclean, Gerald (eds) (1996) *The Spivak Reader*, New York: Routledge.

A collection of Spivak's essays, with introductory summaries to each essay, a short introduction to Spivak, her key terms and ideas, and a new essay. A helpful introductory reader.

McLeod, John (2000) *Beginning Postcolonialism*, Manchester: Manchester University Press.

This book provides a clear overview of postcolonial literature and theory, including some discussion of Spivak's thought, and a range of examples showing how postcolonial theory can be applied in the practice of reading literary texts.

Moore-Gilbert, B.J. (1997) *Postcolonial Theory: Contexts, Practices, Politics*, London: Verso.

This book provides a rigorous historical study of postcolonial theory and criticism from Chinua Achebe to Homi Bhabha. It includes a detailed chapter on Spivak's work that focuses on her work on the subaltern and criticism of western feminism.

Parry, B. (1987) 'Problems in Current Theories of Colonial Discourse', *Oxford Literary Review* 9 (1–2) pp.27–58.

In this article, Parry criticises Spivak for silencing the voice of subaltern resistance in her use of western critical theory.

Shetty, S. and Bellamy E.J. (2000) 'Postcolonialism's Archive Fever', *Diacritics* 30 (1) pp.25–48.

Includes an essay that provides a detailed reading of 'Can the Subaltern Speak?', focusing specifically on the colonial archives discussed in the essay.

Varadharajan, A. (1995) *Exotic Parodies: Subjectivity in Adorno, Said, and Spivak*, Minneapolis: University of Minnesota Press.

This book contains a chapter on Gayatri Spivak which tries to redeem Spivak's thinking from (what Varadharajan suggests is) the abyss of deconstruction via the critical theory of Theodor W. Adorno.

Young, R. (1990) *White Mythologies: Writing History and The West*, Routledge: New York and London.

This book contains a lucid and insightful chapter on Spivak's early thought.

—— (2001) *Postcolonialism: An Historical Introduction* Oxford: Blackwell.

This detailed historical study of anti- and postcolonial thought contains a short, but insightful discussion of Gayatri Spivak and Homi Bhabha, which situates their work in relation to the history of anti-colonial thought, Third World national liberation movements, and the postcolonial revision of Marxism.

INTERNET RESOURCES

For a more detailed list of publications by and about Gayatri Spivak, go to:

<http://sun3.lib.uci.edu/indiv/scctr/Wellek/spivak/index.html>.

WORKS CITED

All the books used as sources for quotations within the text are listed in this section. More detailed information about books and articles by Spivak and their first publication dates can be found in the Further reading section.

Ahmad, A. (1992) *In Theory: Classes, Nations, Literatures*, London: Verso.

Alexander, M.J. and Mohanty C.T. (eds) (1997) *Feminist Genealogies, Colonial Legacies, Democratic Futures*, London and New York: Routledge.

Armstrong, N. (1987) *Desire and Domestic Fiction: A Political History of the Novel*, New York: Oxford University Press.

Bennington, G. (1993) *Jacques Derrida*, Chicago: Chicago University Press.

—— (2000) 'Deconstruction and Ethics', in Nick Royle (ed.) *Deconstructions: A User's Guide*, Houndsmills: Palgrave, pp.64–82.

Bhabha, H. (1994) *The Location of Culture*, London: Routledge.

Bhatt, C. (2001) 'Kant's "raw man" and the miming of primitivism: Spivak's *Critique of Postcolonial Reason*', *Radical Philosophy* 105, pp.37–44.

Butler, J (1993) *Bodies that matter: on the discursive limits of 'sex'*, London and New York: Routledge.

Castree, N. (1996/7) 'Invisible Leviathan: Speculations on Marx, Spivak and the Question of Value', *Rethinking Marxism* 9 (2) pp.45–78.

Chow, R. (1993) *Writing Diaspora: Tactics of Intervention in Contemporary Cultural Studies*, Bloomington and Indianapolis: Indiana University Press.

—— (1993a) 'Ethics after Idealism', *Diacritics* 23 (1) pp.3–22.

—— (1998) *Ethics After Idealism: Theory – Culture – Ethnicity – Reading*, Bloomington and Indianapolis: Indiana University Press.

Conrad, J. (1973) *Heart of Darkness*, Harmondsworth: Penguin.

Critchley, S. (1992) *The Ethics of Deconstruction*, Oxford: Blackwell.

Danius, S. and Jonsson, S. (1993) 'An Interview with Gayatri Chakravorty Spivak', *boundary 2: An International Journal of Literature and Culture*, 20 (2) pp.24–50.

de Man, P. (1983) *Blindness and Insight: Essays in the Rhetoric of Contemporary Criticism*, Minneapolis: University of Minnesota Press.

Derrida, J. (1967) 'Difference' in *Margins of Philosophy*, trans. Alan Bass, Chicago: University of Chicago Press, 1982.

—— (1976) *Of Grammatology*, trans. Gayatri Chakravorty Spivak, Baltimore: Johns Hopkins.

—— (1991) *A Derrida Reader*, Peggy Kamuf (ed.), Hemel Hempstead: Harvester and Wheatsheaf.

—— (1993) *Aporias*, trans. Thomas Dutoit, Stanford: Stanford University Press.

—— (1994) *Specters of Marx: The State of the Debt, the Work of Mourning, and the New International*, trans. Peggy Kamuf, London and New York: Routledge.

—— (1995) *Archive Fever: A Freudian Impression*, trans. E. Prenowitz, Chicago: Chicago University Press.

—— (1999) 'Marx and Sons', trans. G.M. Goshgarian in *Ghostly Demarcations: A Symposium on Jacques Derrida's 'Specters of Marx'*, Michael Sprinker (ed.), London: Verso, pp.213–69.

Devi, M. (1995) *Imaginary Maps*, trans G.C. Spivak, New York: Routledge.

Dirlik, A. 'The Postcolonial Aura: Third World Criticism in the Age of Global Capitalism', *Critical Inquiry* 20, pp.328–56.

Donaldson, L. (1992) *Decolonizing Feminisms: Race, Gender and Empire Building*, Chapel Hill: University of North Carolina.

Eagleton, T. (1999) 'In the Gaudy Supermarket', *London Review of Books* 21 (10) pp.3, 5–6.

Emberley, J. (1993) *Thresholds of Difference: Feminist Critique, Native Women's Writing, Postcolonial Theory*, Toronto: University of Toronto Press.

Fanon, F. (1970) *A Dying Colonialism*, trans. from French by Haakon Chevalier, with foreword by G.M. Carstairs, Harmondsworth: Penguin.

Foucault, M. (1981) *The History of Sexuality. Volume One: An Introduction*, trans. Robert Hurley, Harmondsworth: Penguin.

Fuss, D. (1989) *Essentially Speaking: Feminism, Nature and Difference*, New York and London: Routledge.

Gandhi, L. (1998) *Postcolonial Theory: A Critical Introduction*. New York and Chichester: Columbia University Press.

Gilbert, S. and Gubar, S. (1979) *The Madwoman in the Attic: the Woman Writer and the Nineteenth-Century Literary Imagination*, New Haven: Yale University Press.

Gramsci, A. (1978) *Selections from Prison Notebooks*, trans. Quintin Hoare and Geoffrey Nowell Smith, London: Lawrence and Wishart.

Guha, R. (1983) *Elementary Aspects of Peasant Insurgency in Colonial India*, Delhi: Oxford University Press India.

—— (1988) 'On Some Aspects of the Historiography of Colonial India', in Ranajit Guha and Gayatri Spivak (eds) *Selected Subaltern Studies*, Oxford: Oxford University Press, pp.37–44.

Hall, S. (1988) 'New ethnicities', in Kobena Mercer (ed.) *Black Film, British Cinema*, BFI/ICA Documents 7, pp.21–31.

Hill, J. (1998) 'Crossing the Water: hybridity and ethics in *The Crying Game*', *Textual Practice* 12 (1) pp.89–100.

Hitchcock, P. (1999) *Oscillate Wildly: Space, Body and Spirit of Millennial Materialism*, Minneapolis: University of Minnesota Press.

Irigaray, L. (1985) *This Sex Which is Not One*, trans. Catherine Porter with Carolyn Burke, Ithaca: Cornell University Press.

Katrak, K.H. (1992) 'Indian Nationalism, Gandhian "*Satyagraha*", and Representations of Female Sexuality', in Andrew Parker *et al.* (eds.) *Nationalisms and Sexualities*, London: Routledge, pp.395–406.

Keenan, T. (1997) *Fables of Responsibility: Aberrations and Predicaments in Ethics and Politics*, Stanford: Stanford University Press.

Kristeva, J. (1977) *About Chinese Women*, trans. Anita Barrows, London: Marion Boyars.

Kumar, A. (2000) *Passport Photos*, Berkeley: University of California Press.

Lazarus, N. (1999) *Nationalism and Cultural Practice in the Postcolonial World*, Cambridge: Cambridge University Press.

Levinas, E. (1969) *Totality and Infinity*, trans. Alphonso Lingis, Pittsburgh, PA: Duquesne University Press.

Lowe, L. (1996) *Immigrant Acts: on Asian American Cultural Politics*, Durham: Duke University Press.

Marx, K. (1976) *Capital Volume One*, trans. Ben Fowkes, Harmondsworth: Pelican.

—— (1977) *Karl Marx: Selected Writings* (ed.), David McLellan, Oxford: Oxford University Press.

Medevoi L., Raman S., and Johnson B. (1990) 'Can the Subaltern Vote?', *Socialist Review* 20 (3) pp.133–49.

Mohanty, C.T. (1988) 'Under Western Eyes: Feminist Scholarship and Colonial Discourses', *Feminist Review* 30, pp.65–88.

Moore-Gilbert, B.J. (1997) *Post-Colonial Theory: Contexts, Practices, Politics*, London: Verso.

O'Hanlon, R. (1988) 'Recovering the Subject: Subaltern Studies and Histories of Resistance in Colonial South Asia', *Modern Asian Studies* 22 (1) pp.189–224.

Parker, A. *et al.* (eds) (1992) *Nationalisms and Sexuality*, New York: Routledge.

Parry, B. (1987) 'Problems in Current Theories of Colonial Discourse', *Oxford Literary Review* 9 (1–2) pp.27–58.

Ray, S. (1992) 'Shifting Subjects Shifting Ground: The Names and Spaces of the Postcolonial', *Hypatia* 7 (2) pp.188–201.

Rhys, J. (1996) *Wide Sargasso Sea*, London: Penguin.

Said, E. (1978) *Orientalism: Western Conceptions of the Orient*, Harmondsworth: Penguin.

—— (1983) *The World, the Text, the Critic*, Cambridge, MA, Harvard University Press.

—— (1993) *Culture and Imperialism*, London: Chatto and Windus.

Salgado, M. (2000) 'Tribal Stories, Scribal Worlds', *Journal of Commonwealth Literature* 35 (1) pp.131–45.

Sanders, M. (1999) 'Postcolonial Reading: Review of Gayatri Chakravorty Spivak, *A Critique of Postcolonial Reason: Toward a History of the Vanishing Present*', *Postmodern Culture* 10 (1). Available online at <http://muse.jhu.edu/journals/postmodern_culture/toc/pmc10.1.html>.

Saussure, F. de (1959) *Course in General Linguistics* (eds) C. Bally and A. Sechehaye, New York: McGraw-Hill.

Shetty, S. and Bellamy E.J. (2000) 'Postcolonialism's Archive Fever', *Diacritics* 30 (1) pp.25–48.

Spivak, G.C. (1985) 'Three Women's Texts and a Critique of Imperialism', *Critical Inquiry* 12 (1) pp.243–61.

—— (1985a) 'The Rani of Sirmur: An Essay in Reading the Archives', *History and Theory*, 24 (3) pp.247–72.

—— (1986) 'Imperialism and Sexual Difference', *Oxford Literary Review* 7 (1–2) pp.225–40.

—— (1987) *In Other Worlds: Essays in Cultural Politics*, with a preface by Colin MacCabe, New York: Methuen.

—— (1987a) 'Speculations on Reading Marx: After Reading Derrida', in Derek Attridge *et al.* (eds), *Post-Structuralism and the Question of History*, Cambridge: Cambridge University Press, pp.30–62.

—— (1988) 'Can the Subaltern Speak?', in Cary Nelson and Lawrence Grossberg (eds) *Marxism and the Interpretation of Culture*, London: Macmillan, pp.271–313.

—— (1990) *The Post-Colonial Critic: Interviews, Strategies, Dialogues*, Sarah Harasym (ed.), New York and London: Routledge.

—— (1991) Theory in the Margin: Coetzee's *Foe* Reading Defoe's *Crusoe/Roxana*', in Jonathan Arac and Barbara Johnson (eds) *Consequences of Theory: Selected Papers of the English Institute, 1987–88*, Baltimore: Johns Hopkins University Press, 1990, pp.154–80.

—— (1992) 'Woman in Difference: Mahasweta Devi's "Douloti the Bountiful"', in Andrew Parker *et al.* (eds) *Nationalisms and Sexuality*, New York: Routledge, pp.96–120.

—— (1993) *Outside in the Teaching Machine*, New York and London: Routledge.

—— (1993a) 'An Interview with Gayatri Chakravorty Spivak', Sara Danius and Stefan Jonsson, *boundary 2*, 20 (2) pp.24–50.

—— (1994) 'Responsibility', *boundary 2*, 21 (3) pp.19–64.

—— (1995) 'Ghostwriting', *Diacritics*, 25 (2) pp.65–84.

—— (1995a) 'Supplementing Marxism', in Steven Cullenberg and Bernd Magnus (eds) *Whither Marxism?*, New York: Routledge, pp. 109–19.

—— (1995b) 'Three Women's Texts and a Critique of Imperialism', revised extract in Fred Botting (ed.) *Frankenstein*, London: Macmillan New Casebooks, pp.235–60.

—— (1996) *The Spivak Reader*, Donna Landry and Gerald Maclean (eds), New York and London: Routledge.

—— (1996a) 'Transnationality and the Multiculturalist Ideology: Interview with Gayatri Chakravorty Spivak', in Deepika Bahri and Mary Vasudeva (eds) *Between the Lines: South Asians and Postcoloniality*, Philadelphia: Temple University Press, 1996, pp.64–88.

—— (1998) 'Setting to Work of Deconstruction', in Michael Kelly (ed.) *Encyclopedia of Aesthetics Volume Two*, Oxford: Oxford University Press, 4 vols, pp.7–11.

—— (1999) *A Critique of Postcolonial Reason: Towards a History of the Vanishing Present*, Cambridge, MA: Harvard University Press.

—— (2000) 'Schmitt and Poststructuralism: a Response', *Cardozo Law Review* 21 (5–6), May pp.1723–37.

—— (2001) 'A Note on the New International', *parallax* 7 (3) pp.12–16.

Subaltern Studies: Writings on South Asian History and Society (1982–99) vols. I–X, Guha, R. *et al.* (eds) Delhi: Oxford University Press India.

Varadharajan, A. (1995) *Exotic Parodies: Subjectivity in Adorno, Said, and Spivak*, Minneapolis: University of Minnesota Press.

Viswanathan, G. (1987) *Masks of Conquest: Literary Study and British Rule in India*, London: Faber.

Visweswaran, K. (1994) *Fictions of Feminist Ethnography*, Minneapolis and London: University of Minnesota Press.

Wales, K. (1989) *A Dictionary of Stylistics*, London and New York: Longman.

Young, R. (2001) *Postcolonialism: An Historical Introduction*, Oxford: Blackwell.

—— (1995) *'Colonial Desire': Hybridity in Theory, Culture and Race*, London: Routledge.

—— (1990) *White Mythologies: Writing History and The West*, New York and London: Routledge.

INDEX

Achebe, Chinua 123
A Critique of Postcolonial Reason 16, 114, 135
Adorno, Theodor 5, 23, 41, 139
aesthetic representation 57, 58
Ahmad, Aijaz 15, 112
Algerian war of independence 29, 77
Alexander, M. Jacqui 139
'A Literary Representation of the Subaltern' 17, 21, 39, 124
Althusser, Louis 92, 104
Amin, Samir 93
Amin, Shahid 49
'A Note on the New International' 43
anti-colonial insurgency 33, 39
anti-essentialism 73
aporia 27
Armstrong, Nancy: *Desire and Domestic Fiction* 86
Arnold, David 49

Balibar, Etienne 104
Bandung conference 94

Barthes, Roland 17
Bataille, Georges 106
Baudrillard, Jean 106
Beauvoir, Simone de 72–4
Bellamy, Elizabeth Jane 68, 140
Benjamin, Walter 105
Bennington, Geoffrey 34
Bhabha, Homi 1, 15, 27, 29, 31, 32, 61, 111, 136: 'Sly Civility' 30; 'DissemiNation' 30
Bhaduri, Bhubaneswari 33, 41, 64, 65, 66
Bhatt, Chetan 117
binary oppositions 25
British Empire 3, 39, 48, 62, 88, 98, 130
Bronte, Charlotte: *Jane Eyre* 10, 86–89, 111, 116–20
Butler, Judith 73–4, 104, 138

'Can the Subaltern Speak?' 9, 21, 35, 41, 56, 57, 62–8, 71, 88, 135, 139
capitalism 10, 106, 108

Castree, Noel 137
catachresis 34, 35
categorical imperative 117
Chatterjee, Partha 2, 49, 124
chiasmus 41, 122
Chow, Rey 8, 22, 47, 108, 137
Cixous, Héléne 71, 74
clitoridectomy 10, 83, 89
Coetzee, J.M. 11: *Foe* 10, 120–3
colonial archives 4, 60
colonial discourse 19, 61, 85, 88,
  111–2, 118, 123, 135
colonial education 3, 28, 122
colonialism 1, 2, 9, 10, 20, 27, 29,
  45, 49, 111, 113
colonised 33, 45
Conrad, Joseph 19
Cornell, Drucilla 135
Critchley, Simon 38, 43
critical interruption 20–1
critical theory 1, 2, 7, 15, 23, 32,
  42, 105, 135
continuous sign chain 54
counter-globalist development
  activism 43, 44

death 27
decolonisation 39, 40, 50, 129
deconstruction 4, 5, 18, 20, 33, 39,
  40, 48, 53, 105, 108, 110, 113:
  definition, 26–7; and postcolonial
  theory 31; political value of 35;
  ethics 36, 41, 43; affirmative
  deconstruction 42, 44; and
  Marxism 94–6, 134
Defoe, Daniel: *Robinson Crusoe* 111,
  120–2
Deleuze, Gilles 9, 56–8
Derrida, Jacques 4, 17, 21, 24, 25,
  26–7, 29, 38, 39, 42, 52, 55, 56,
  94, 95, 96, 103, 109, 127,
  137–8: textuality 18, 23, 25;

différance 26, 29; supplement 26;
  and Algeria 29; criticism of
  Claude Lévi Strauss 32; proper
  name 34; political thinking 36
Descartes, René 26
development studies 25
Devi, Mahasweta 7, 71, 112, 136:
  'Breast Giver' 7–8 39, 47, 75–6,
  84, 124–6, 130; 'Pterodactyl,
  Pirtha and Puran Sahay' 43, 128;
  'Draupadi' 55, 131–2; 'Douloti
  the Bountiful' 98, 128, 130
Devi, Phoolan 66, 112
Dirlik, Arif 15, 136
Djebar, Assia 112, 138
discourse 19, 85, 86, 104
Donaldson, Laura 138

Eagleton, Terry 16, 21
East India Company 19, 60, 61,
  78, 111
economic determinism 104–5
elite nationalism 54
English literature, 3
Emberley, Julia 138
epistemic violence 19
epistemology 19
essentialism 73
ethics 35, 36–7, 43, 108, 127,
  140
exchange value 101–4

Fanon, Frantz 2, 20, 23, 77,
  123
feminism 20, 21, 22, 28, 39,
  40, 71–84, 87, 89, 90, 91,
  141: Marxist feminism 76,
  125–6; French feminism;
  transnational feminism
feminist literary criticism 87
'Feminism and Critical Theory' 21,
  71, 74, 97

'First World' 2, 5, 8, 15, 21, 27, 28, 29, 84, 91, 101, 105, 106, 107, 109, 131

Foucault, Michel 9, 17, 21, 56–8, 85, 86, 104

French feminism 71, 72, 83, 84

'French Feminism in an International Frame' 10, 21, 71, 74, 78–84, 87, 89–90

Freud, Sigmund 17, 28, 81

Gandhi, Indira 61

Gandhi, Leela 123

Gandhi, Mohandas Karamchand 6, 20, 39, 125

Gates, Henry Louis 73

General Agreement on Trade and Tariffs (GATT) 109

Gilbert, Sandra and Susan Gubar: *The Madwoman in the Attic* 86, 117

global capitalism 15, 18, 21, 92, 96, 99, 104, 106–7, 135, 137, 141

globalisation 5, 9, 104, 135

Goux, Jean Joseph 106

Gramsci, Antonio 46, 47, 48, 49, 65

Grosz, Elizabeth 18, 20, 28

Guha, Ranajit 6, 48, 49, 50, 59

Hall, Stuart 75, 104

Handsworth Songs (film) 30

Haraway, Donna 104

Hardiman, David 49

Harvey, David 93

Heart of Darkness 19

Hegel, G.W.F. 16, 99–100, 135

hegemony: (definition) 65

Heidegger, Martin 28, 42

Hill, John 127–8

Hitchcock, Peter 137

humanism 72

humanist subject 29

idealism 99–100

ideology 65, 101, 104

immigrant 1, 31

imperialism 3, 141: as civilising mission 63, 112, 117, 120; axiomatics of imperialism 114, 116

'Imperialism and Sexual Difference' 21, 40, 111

India 2, 3, 6, 28, 30, 32, 46, 49, 54, 55, 113, 125, 129; communist party 51, 52; Congress Party 52, 61, Mutiny 66

In Other Worlds 20, 60

indigenous parties 52

international division of labour 2, 9, 10, 27, 91–8, 101, 104–5, 109

Iranian revolution 77

Irigaray, Luce 71, 74

Jameson, Fredric 104

Jayawardena, Kumari 72

Johnson, Benjamin 67

Kant, Immanuel 10, 112, 114–117, 135

Katrak, Ketu H. 125

Keenan, Thomas 95, 135, 137

Kofman, Sarah 36

Kristeva, Julia 10, 71, 74: *About Chinese Women* 79–82, 86

Kumar, Amitava 137

Kureishi, Hanif 2, 112

Lacan, Jacques 81

Laclau, Ernesto 4, 92, 93, 104

Lacoue Labarthe, Phillipe 36

Lazarus, Neil 54, 59

Lenin, Vladimir 51

Levinas, Emmanuel 37, 42

Lévi Strauss, Claude 17, 32

'Limits and Openings of Marx in Derrida' 36
Literature 111
Livingstone, David 19
Lowe, Lisa 137

MacCabe, Collin 20
Macaulay, Thomas Babington 3
Mahabharata 132
Makhmalbaf, Mohsen: *Kandahar* 77
Man, Paul de 3–4, 113–14
Marx, Karl 10, 17, 49, 57, 91–110: labour theory of value 21, 22, 91, 94, 101–2, 107, 110; double meaning of representation in 57; ideology 92; colonialism and 93, 97; Eurocentrism, 94; commodity 101–2; on *Robinson Crusoe* 120–1, 135
Marxism 15, 18, 20, 22, 32, 35, 39, 42, 45, 51–3, 93, 97, 109, 141
master words 34, 35, 45
materialism 99–100
Medevoi, Leerom 67
Mill, John Stuart 30
Mohanty, Chandra Talpade 71, 75, 77, 78, 139
Moore Gilbert, Bart 15, 16, 61, 66, 112–3, 139–40
Mother India mythology 39–40, 47, 125, 129
Mouffe, Chantal 92
multinational corporations 28, 72, 97
multinational capitalism 31, *see also* global capitalism

Nambikwara 32
Nancy, Jean Luc 36

national independence 1, 20, 32, 35, 39, 45, 52, 94, 122, 124, 129: and India 6, 7, 40, 48, 49, 50, 52, 60, 66, 98–9, 125; elitism 50, 51, 54, 130
nationalism 15, 124: anti-colonial nationalism 2, 48
neocolonialism 9
Nicaragua 67
Nietzsche, Friedrich 28

Of Grammatology 25, 38–9, 55, 103
O'Hanlon, Rosalind 53
Orientalism 38, 85, 112
other 37, 38, 42, 116, 128, 140
Outside in the Teaching Machine 36

Pandey, Gyanendra 49
Parry, Benita 32, 66, 127, 139
peasant insurgency 52, 53
political representation 57, 58
Pontecorvo, Gillo: *The Battle of Algiers* 77–8
Porter, Roy 112
postcolonial criticism 25, 112–3, 141
postcolonial intellectual 8, 31, 46, 58, 137
postcolonial studies 8, 38
postcolonial subject 1, 29
postcolonial texts 112, 113, 118, 120, 123, 128
postcolonial theory 1, 7, 10, 15, 16, 137; deconstruction and 31
poststructuralism 21, 58
proletariat 34, 45, 56

Rajan, Gita 61
Rajan, Rajeswari Sunder 71
Raman, Shankar 67
'The Rani of Sirmur' 60–1, 71, 111
Ray, Sangeeta 136

'Responsibility' 42
Rhys, Jean: *Wide Sargasso Sea* 10, 11, 86, 88–9, 119–20
Roy, M.N. 51
rural peasantry 3, 6, 47, 49, 50; Naxalbari peasant rebellion 50, 52, 55, 56
Rushdie, Salman 112

Saadawi, Nawal El 71
Said, Edward 1, 4, 15, 38, 62, 85, 86, 93, 111–2, 118, 120, 136: on style 16; Spivak's critique of 17
Salgado, Minoli 126–7
Sassen, Saskia 137
sati 62–4, 65, 66, 89, 140
Saussure, Ferdinand de 17, 26
'Scattered Speculations on the Question of Value' 21, 98, 101
'The Setting to Work of Deconstruction' 42
Shakespeare, William 19
Shelley, Mary: *Frankenstein* 86, 111, 128
Shetty, Sandhya 69, 140
Spivak, Gayatri Chakravorty: place in postcolonial studies 1–2; early life 2–3; style 5–6, 9; institutional location 8, worlding 18; 'Translator's Preface to *Of Grammatology* 9, 22, 25, 27–8, 31; rejection of the term postcolonial 123
strategic essentialism 74–5
structuralism 17
subaltern 6, 10, 23, 32, 42, 43, 44, 45, 46, 49, 50, 52, 55, 56, 128, 137; definition 47; subaltern subject effect 54; subaltern woman 59, 60, 61, 62, 65, 67, 71, 99, 107, 124, 126, 130

Subaltern Studies 6, 47, 48, 56: Spivak's critique of 7, 46, 47, 49, 51, 53
sublime 115
surplus value 101

terra nullius 19
terrorism 140
textuality 19
The Tempest 19
Thiongo, Ngugi wa 123
'Third World' 15, 21, 22, 27, 29, 44, 58, 74, 77, 89, 94, 101, 105–10, 131–133, 137
Third World intellectuals 28
Third World political thought 20
Third World women 2, 7, 8, 9, 21, 25, 28, 40, 55, 59, 61, 71–84, 96, 107, 100, 138
Third World workers 28
Thompson, Edward 63
'Three Women's Texts and a Critique of Imperialism' 3, 10, 40, 84–90, 111, 116, 118, 128

United Nations 138–9
USA 2, 31, 78
use value 100–104, 107

value 10, 91, 100, 103, 106
Varadharajan, Asha 40–1, 139
Viswanathan, Gauri 111
Visweswaran, Kamala 138

women, 3, 6, 33–4, 35, 45, 54, 74, 97, 139
worker 33–4, 35, 45, 97–8, 100, 104
Woolf, Virginia 4
Wordsworth, William 4

worlding 18–19
World Bank 18, 42
World Trade Organisation (WTO)
  18, 109

Yeats, W.B. 3
Young, Robert J.C. 3, 15, 16, 21–2,
  27, 29, 41, 51, 52, 93, 109, 136,
  139